KISSES OUT OF THE BLUE

KISSES OUT OF THE BLUE

Twenty-Two Life-Embracing Stories
from the Dead, Inanimate Objects,
Star Brothers, Geese,
and Other Unlikely Sources

by

LINDA GNAT-MULLIN

BROOKLYN, NEW YORK

2014

Cover and interior design: Michael Gnat
Cover photo: Andy Roberts, Getty Images
Author photo: Kit Kaplan

Printed in the United States of America
Published in Brooklyn, New York

Linda Gnat-Mullin
Kisses Out of the Blue
172 Fifth Avenue, #240
Brooklyn, NY 11217
energeticempowerment.org

For author-inscribed copies, quantity discounts, workshops, readings, and more, contact the author at lindagnatmullin@gmail.com.

Publisher's Cataloging-in-Publication Data

Gnat-Mullin, Linda M.
   Kisses out of the blue : twenty-two life-embracing stories from the dead, inanimate objects, star brothers, geese, and other unlikely sources / Linda Gnat-Mullin.
     p.   cm.
     ISBN 978-0-615-87037-3

1. Gnat-Mullin, Linda M.   2. Spiritual biography.   3. Mediums—United States—Biography.   4. Angels—Anecdotes.   5. Reincarnation—Biography.   6. Self-actualization—Anecdotes.   I. Kisses out of the blue : twenty-two life-embracing stories from the dead, inanimate objects, star brothers, geese, and other unlikely sources.   II. Title.

BL53.G585 2013
291.4/2/92—dc23   2013915565

With love and gratitude to . . .

Wonderful Husband, Amazing Son
Dear Mother, Father, Sister, Brother
Great (+ Great Big) Family
Watchful Ancestors
Patient Friends
Inspiring Reiki Teachers and Masters
Fellow Healing Facilitators
Avid Students and Clients and Readers
(Especially You!)
Past, Present, and Future
and Those Who Guide Us All.

Contents

Acknowledgments   *page* ix

Author's Note: Why Do You Have This Little
Tiny Book?   1

1. Everything Is Observed   5
2. Nice Trumps Knavery   9
3. What Flows from the Heart?   15
4. Help Comes   19
5. Nothing Doesn't Respond   23
6. Timing Counts   29
7. In the Middle of a Phone Call   33
8. Generous Nature   37
9. Give It All You've Got, Then Give It Over   41
10. There Can Be Refuge   45
11. The Karmic Energy Commission Newsletter   51
12. Animals Get It   57

CONTENTS

13. Go for the Cheeseburger   61
14. We're Not Nearly Alone   65
15. Gang Aft Agley   71
16. Lively Lessons from the Deceased   75
17. All Time Is Now   79
18. Past Tense   85
19. Break It Up   95
20. Messages Are Everywhere   101
21. Grab a Pocketful of Change   107
22. Give Yourself Your Self   119

The X Factor: Eleven Ways to Be Kissed and
        Tell It!   129
Before You Go: One Last Kiss   133
Finally: Embrace It All   137

Acknowledgments

Thanks beyond thanks to . . .

Debra K. Crist
        Nettie Paisley
                Shyda Hoque
                        Stacy Cavanaugh
                                Jeffrey Gustavson
                                        Martin Edmunds

Michael Gnat
        David Parker
                David Oz
                        Anthony Vigorito
                              Laurie Graff
                                  Nathan P.
                                        Duane Baby

Why Do You Have This Little Tiny Book?

You'll find out. It's no accident that you are reading this sentence. Or this fragment.

In these pages, you'll meet a number of spirits, contentious poultry, women on the verge of a feminist breakthrough, a handful of time travelers, a few bandits, an angel or two, a brilliant master chef, annoyed British servants, and some possible star brothers, among others. Every story I've written is, to the best of my perception, absolutely true. Where appropriate, names have been changed and identifying details omitted.

These tales tap into the higher levels of reality, above every distraction this planet delivers. It's where we are so easily connected to all that is, where time and space and perceived identity are no barriers to healing and love. (And kisses.) Many stories involve intuition. Yet there's nothing I'm doing intuitively that you can't do. It's your birthright.

I believe that everything we do is recorded in light for all time. Be careful in your choices. Otherwise, you might find yourself, like me, lying on a musty hummingbird-hued carpet in Mexico in 1984, wailing deeply (I'm not a big crier) about a deed I did a thousand years before that seemed kind of fun at the time. I started amending my actions in bits and pieces in 2001; I'm stretching toward more freedom.

This kind of talk isn't coming from some lifelong choir member. For nearly thirty years, I worked in advertising, where I wrote copy rapidly and amorally, creating direct mail for medical insurance that scared old people; helping introduce plastic grocery bags to the United States; promoting the F-22 and delivery systems for weapons of mass destruction; and, worst of all, selling heaps of porcelain collectibles. I had put aside my fragile authentic self that loved intuition and healing and created this other self for whom pleasing the client was the only acceptable aspiration. I frankly didn't see how the healer could live in this world.

At a certain point, I had transient global amnesia, wherein my brain locked up for about thirty-six hours. I went somewhere else, perhaps to an intense discussion about how I was squandering my life. When I came back, all I knew was that I had to change.

My effort is far from perfect. It is, I believe, going in a decent direction. Writing this book for you is part of it. Toward the end of these twenty-two stories, I'll offer suggestions for you about how you can experience more and more kisses from the universe.

Meanwhile, imagine (or YouTube) the celestial Dinah Shore, in black-and-white or color, singing to the good people of "the greatest land of all." As she sings, her right hand makes a fist and then relaxes a little, again and again, until, at last, she opens it fully, like a fragrant blossom, presses it to her lips, and blows you a generous "M-WAH!"

A kiss from me.

ONE

Everything Is Observed

For many years, my grandfather Charlie ran what we called "The Poultry House." It wasn't a home for poultry, it was a place where people came and bought fresh chickens, geese, and ducks, all culled from small farms within about a fifty-mile radius of the store.

These animals had spent their lives in gravel-filled chicken yards, running around, crowing and clucking, being fed corn and food scraps out of big, white, scarred, enamel basins. Had my grandfather lived in the twenty-first century, he would have been part of a movement. In his era, he was just making a living.

Every animal was brought to the back of the store live, killed with one blow, and dressed on the spot. The word "dressing" actually connotes *un*dressing. The inside was cleaned out. The feathers were removed carefully, so the skin would be smooth and appealing.

In 1928, Herbert Hoover campaigned on the slogan "A Chicken in Every Pot," and my grandfather was the man with the chickens. Throughout the Great Depression, he was able to feed his growing family. During the Second World War, housewives brought in their ration stamps, bit their bright lips, and hoped for the best. But in the 1950s, things changed.

The first supermarkets opened, the poultry house got smaller and then closed. The brass pendulum of the octagonal clock on the wall was stopped after years of service. My grandfather joined my father in a new wave—the do-it-yourselfer. They started renting tools to the homeowners who bought fixer-uppers after the war. They introduced the wonders of the first power lawn mowers and grew from there.

Through the years, my grandfather had been exuberant about life, and a bit of a jokester. One day, after making his chicken rounds, he brought home a cow's head and slipped it into the icebox, just to shock his wife and children. He taught his little granddaughters how to be flower girls for the many weddings in our large family, giving them baskets of torn-up newspaper for practice. He ate butter on coffee cake with the gusto of his Alsatian roots—you could see a full dental impression where he took a bite. And at Christmastime, when he opened a present, he always shouted, "Hooray!"

This was remarkable, especially with all he had suffered in childhood—the early loss of his father, an artist and engraver; the subsequent depression of his mother; their economic struggles; the death of a little sister at age six in the early 1900s . . . so hidden in the bosom of family memory, I did not know of or see an image of her until almost a century later.

Time went on; my grandfather retired, wore bolo ties, died. His memorial service was in the chapel of a large cemetery. It was an occasion filled with light and appreciative laughter.

But when the guests filed out of the chapel, they discovered a phalanx of geese right at the entryway. The geese began to hiss and charge and nip with remarkable focus and dedication; people had to dodge and run in their somber, constricting clothes, Sunday lace-up Oxfords, and black high heels.

"Hey Charlie," a son shouted to the back-lit cumulus sky, "it's the revenge of the poultry!"

We'll never know for sure if Charlie watched it happen—or made it happen.

TWO

Nice Trumps Knavery

Once upon a time—1970, actually—I worked as a drawing-room maid in a stately home that shall remain unnamed, in a part of England that shall remain unmentioned. This large country house was situated on a finely manicured lawn that transitioned into woodlands. In the private garden were deep green topiary shrubs cut into perfect angles, accented with little scarlet blossoms that barely dared blow in the wind. Tiny bits of mica in the golden-gray stone walls glimmered on a summer's day, and sunlight sparkled off the floor-length mullioned windows. As to the mistress of the house, it's enough to say that she was near the pinnacle of society.

Her home overflowed with treasures, including set after set of priceless French porcelain painted with exotic birds and flowers bounded by bright bands of color embossed with gold. There were jewel-toned settees with golden lion paws for feet. And many paintings of ancestors, their gleaming eyes gazing out into the mote-filled light. One pale lady had spent 500 years showing off her pretty, tapering fingers loaded with onyx rings.

Among the artifacts was a Victorian armchair carved entirely of ivory. (Yes, I know—a damnable object. It was a gift, however, which excuses nothing but may explain something.) I was brushing it clean one day when one arm fell off and clattered to the floor. My face turned the color of the chair. An old man on the cleaning staff saw my dilemma, gently pressed the arm back into place and kindly said, "Not to worry. Happens all the time. Off you go."

The staff pub in the basement was overseen by a Scottish publican with crazy black hair. He loved country music and "Mahty Rhobbens." The staff would gather to gossip, especially on weeks when there were overnight guests to care for. I sipped Babycham, its label featuring a cartoon of a wide-eyed fawn.

It was there that I learned how we servants could tell people with no true gentility, no class. You wouldn't see it in their clothes, which might be the richest of woolens or evening gowns light as rose petals. It wasn't their hair, even if it reflected the bright highlights and daring angles of London's latest style maker. Nothing was apparent in the premium cigarettes they pulled from gold-trimmed packets, or the smooth, shining, sweeping lines of the cars they drove.

It was ugly guest behavior toward the servants that was considered by us to be utterly parvenu. Brie-eating smiles in public; vulgar, unkind, unreasonable demands of the staff behind closed doors. Everybody below stairs knew when guests behaved badly. Information traveled quickly. What I wondered was if it ever had a vertical trajectory.

One night in the pub, I, alas, did not want to hear the latest on the rotten guests as I was suffering from my own social miscalculations. I had been assigned to work the coat check area for a dance. All I had to do was to stand near one stone step on a stone floor and indicate gently with my arm and my inside voice, "This way, please," motioning them toward the flower-filled ballroom that lay just beyond. What could possibly go wrong?

Things did go fine for a while with my ushering, and then along came the next guest: an ancient man. If I calculate today, he was born sometime between the Second Boer War and the start of World War I. He had that tortoiselike quality of some old people who hunch over a bit, head barely poking out of an oversized collar as if about to retract. This old man, he took one step wrong and started to weave back and forth. I moved to block his fall. There was a gasp from the immediately assembled—staff and guests alike. The old man caught himself, coughed into midspace, straightened his tie, and moved on.

I honestly don't remember what happened next. At some point, I was below stairs and someone in authority on staff told me, not unkindly but very very firmly: "You must never, EVER touch an aristocrat!" It turned out that the collective gasp was not about that old man's potential fall onto stone, but my possible physical contact with him. This rule was so ingrained, no one had ever thought to mention it.

It was a bitter pill to swallow. I was washing it down with Babycham.

As the servants quaffed their drinks in the pub and waited for a signal from upstairs, some cast sidewise glances at me. They'd all been pretty cordial, but now I feared that they were whispering something to the effect of: "Stupid gringo!"

The personal maid to the lady of the house started to say something, stopped herself, and then finally spoke in her sweet, clear Scottish voice. "I want to tell you," she said in a way that quieted some of the others, "that my lady is always very grateful for everything we do. For all our efforts. She always says 'please' and 'thank you.' She has not an unkind word for anyone. She is always quite appreciative. Even when her hair is washed and styled, she is thankful. And that is the absolute truth."

And with that, the maid took a sip of her Spanish sherry, and let those words hang in the air.

That revelation was a revolution. For this maid was legendarily loyal and protective. Never had I heard the tiniest tidbit of information drop from her lips. In saying this, by her own standards, she might as well have flung a Molotov cocktail into the staff dining room. Or the upstairs one, for that matter. She told me that a woman with everything was grateful for simple things, and for what we did. And she capped it off with the homely image of the great lady herself in curlers. A little miracle of grace.

It was healing balm for a pie-faced girl from the heartland who was deeply ashamed of her ignorance and yet furious at a class distinction that seemed to deny humanity.

In fact, the whole thing was a gift. I received a boo-boo in a war where some people sustained a constant daily barrage. No wonder America was burning down, as some of the staffers cheerfully informed me at breakfast every day. "You're well out of it," they said. But I had just the tiniest taste of being in it.

There—a secret told, another rule broken, but for the greater good. She told it to me, an awkward and impressionable young American working in a great house in 1970, and now I've told you.

THREE

What Flows from the Heart?

In 2007, I set out to teach a little evening course in intuitive development. My meeting place was a grade school classroom in the West Village. The moment I walked in, I was home. There were pictures of blue kachinas dancing on the wall. There was a big map of the Four Corners area of the United States, as realized by fifth graders. Images from indigenous cultures all around. Every week, the classroom was more beautiful.

The adults who came to my course all had some intuitive ability, mostly underused. Some of them had found that their sensitivity had played merry hell with their popularity at school as kids. Now, they had a chance to develop it and enjoy it. There was a new topic announced every week. Each class was drop-in and by donation. Anyone who came wanted to be there.

One week, we worked with water. Dr. Masaru Emoto's book was a sensation; it suggested that water could both be affected by and be a carrier of specific information. The book was profusely illustrated with macro photos of frozen water in crystalline form: some from sources around the world; some that had "listened" to music; and some exposed to inspiring or disturbing words or phrases written in Japanese or English. These various influences seemed to affect the symmetry, size, and beauty of the water crystals.

I decided that we would do a water tasting in class. Five days before, I bought eight bottles of Poland Spring water, and attached one-word messages, all in capital letters, to six of them, so the water could "read" them, just as shown in the book. These were words such as LOVE, JOY, MISSION, GOD, and other high-minded concepts. To be somewhat scientific, I would also have used negative words or phrases on some of the bottles, but I chose not to. Why add to the difficulties of the day?

The two remaining bottles were exposed to classical music, one to Mozart and one to Bach. Both excerpts were the same length and played three times. Then, a label with the name of the musical composition was taped to the appropriate bottle. All the bottles were then stored in a quiet place in my house.

On class day, when it was time for the tasting, I handed out note pads. I opened one bottle of water at a time, passing out dental-rinse-sized cups of that water. I asked each person to write a description of the taste, anything that came to mind as they sipped it, any feelings they might have had. Then, everyone around the table spoke, and finally, I revealed the idea the bottle—and presumably the water—had held, generally to both amusement and amazement, and sometimes rueful laughter. Then, I opened the next bottle and repeated the process.

I was surprised to see that water that had originated from one source could elicit so many different responses. No one was consistently positive or negative about all the bottles.

Finally, the last bottle was opened. Four people described the water as tasting "sweet," "balanced," "soft," "full." The fifth person grimaced. "Uuugh!" she hissed through her teeth, "That is the most disgusting water I ever tasted! It's horrible!" After her remarks, the rest of the descriptions continued to be fairly placid and positive.

And then came the reveal: the piece by Bach that the water had "heard." The woman who hadn't liked the water shrieked. We turned to her. "What is it?" I asked. "That," she said, "is my father's favorite piece of classical music. And I cannot *stand* my father!"

FOUR

Help Comes

When I was a kid, I always felt a little connection with the actor Anthony Perkins. Not a grand schoolgirl crush, just a tiny bond of sorts. He had starred in the film *Friendly Persuasion,* a story of Quakers from Indiana. We had Quakers in my ancestral line, and I was proud.

I had been given a worn hi-fi LP he had recorded called "From My Heart" when my Dad bought a pile of albums from an acquaintance down on his luck. I repeatedly listened to Tony's quiet rendition of "Ole Buttermilk Sky," also written by a Hoosier, despite a popping sound at every revolution.

And, when I had to take Home Economics, and cut out and sew a garment, I passed up the dainty floral print fabrics most girls chose for their self-belted shirt-waists, and opted instead for a moody greenish abstract pattern that stated, "Designed by Anthony Perkins" on the selvage.

So it was a treat a few years ago to meet a young client with a connection to the Perkins family, and to discover that she had often heard and seen Mr. Perkins in spirit. In fact, he seemed to have quite a lot to say. All of which is private, and can't be revealed.

But that wasn't the end of my connection. One day, I was working with a different client who was seeking a Reiki treatment for anxiety.

It came to me from nowhere: the idea that she had seen a lot of horror movies as a child. Maybe she had been dropped off at the movie theater. And so I asked rather than suggested—that's the way I find it's best to proceed with intuitive flashes. She affirmed this.

I suddenly got a mental flash of Tony Perkins himself sitting just beyond my Reiki table, just behind the head of my client.

Taking Tony's cue, I asked, "Do you mean movies like *Psycho*?" She indicated that that was scariest of all. I offered her Reiki to raise her own energy field's vibration so she could very gently release some of the energy of terror. After that, the energy was lighter all around her, and she relaxed.

As the energy flowed I got another mental flash and saw Tony Perkins assume the mien of an old-time Yankee bookkeeper. He had a tiny notebook in one hand, a stubby pencil in the other. He licked his finger, opened a page, made a mark, squinted, then looked in my direction with a twinkle in his eye that seemed both mischievous and rueful. "One down," he said, "64,999 to go." And he vanished.

I didn't tell her then that it had been an archetypal or spirit Tony Perkins who had come to her aid. It seemed to me that in that moment, it would have been counterproductive.

But, when you ask for help, you might just be amazed at where it can come from!

FIVE

Nothing Doesn't Respond

Lucky me. I had been living for twelve years with a battered, scarred kitchen the color of old creamed liver. It looked as if a young Cub Scout troop gone rogue had taken to it with small, round-edged scissors.

I didn't have the talent to renovate it seriously myself, nor the pocketbook for someone else to do it. So, I took a breath and did what I could to fix it up. Then a young, talented man mysteriously appeared who would make the space lovely within my budget. There were wainscoted walls in a soft, buttery color. A ceramic tile backsplash I helped design. The prettiest floor. It became a room that simply radiated light.

It was a miracle, a dream come true, and the final thing we wanted . . . was a pair of Windsor chairs. We looked, but there was nothing that properly combined price range, durability, and visual grace. Two out of three wasn't enough. So, we forgot about it for a while.

One day, in walked the young man with two chairs he had found on the curb a block away. They were indeed Windsor chairs, slightly worn on the seats, but in the very warm, golden honey tone I was looking for, and they were strong, and they were free.

As he carried them in by their arched backs they seemed just fine, but when I set them in place, they looked strangely blocky, exaggerated, really unattractive, as if they were in an old black-and-white Depression-era animated cartoon, about to dance around in a ramshackle barn while some cow played the tuba. I couldn't figure it out.

Finally, it hit me . . . these chairs were carrying the energy of the person who, for whatever reason, put them out on the curb. How long had this person looked at those chairs and thought of replacing them?

So, I got out some lemon oil, took the chairs into the pantry, and began to shine them with the fragrant finish. I told them how beautiful and graceful they were, how we had been waiting for them and were looking forward to putting them in the kitchen.

And then I set them back in place. They were still a little worn, but now they were charming, and blended harmoniously with the room. Sunlight sparkled through their rungs.

It's said that since everything is made of energy, everything has some form of consciousness. André Gregory, in the film *My Dinner with André*, talks about the famed New Age community of Findhorn, Scotland: "Everything they do, they do beautifully," he says, "The buildings just shine. . . . Helen the ice box, the stove, the car, they all have names. . . . You wouldn't treat Helen with any less respect than Margaret, your wife."

I know very clearly that an object carries pictures of where it has been. People who can tap into that information are doing psychometry, that is, reading an object and describing its present and former environments. I once tried to trick a psychometrist by offering two pearl earrings that looked like a pair, but were not. The fronts were identical; the clips on the back were nearly the same, except that one set of clips had a few minuscule etched lines. I nestled the earrings in my hand, clips hidden, and said, "Tell me about these earrings." He immediately separated them and described where each earring came from—and he was right.

If human-made objects can respond, imagine the possibilities of the animate world. Just because something is silent doesn't mean it has nothing to say.

I've even had a knee communicate with me directly. It was a left knee, and it belongs to a lovely, feisty, warmhearted Irish-American Brooklynite of a certain age. Her knee said to me, "Tell her I'm sorry for messing up her nice dress."

Naturally, I hesitated a bit, but the knee insisted. So, I told her. She looked at me for a moment, as if she was weighing my sanity and hers as well for being on my table, but then she simply said, "I don't know what that means." I said, "Well, OK, let's go on." And so we did.

A few minutes later, she pointed a ring-bedecked finger at the air and said, "I've got it. I remember now. On the day of my First Communion, I was all dressed up in my white, lacy dress and veil, and I fell down on the sidewalk and skinned my knee pretty badly. There was blood all over the hem of my dress."

We told the knee it was forgiven.

You may not want to name the contents of your house, nor the toes of your left foot, but it is my theory that anything that is treated kindly is going to look better and perform better than if it is treated with derision or indifference. I speak softly to my washer and dryer, and try not to slam their doors; I am grateful to my stove, which as of this writing is thirty years old.

My printer is twelve years old, which is much older in techie years. Last year, I had a question about it, and someone on the manufacturer's technical support team stated rather forcefully into the phone, "Your printer is obsolete! Replace it!" I was sorry they were having a bad day wherever they were, but refused to let it sway me. I just keep talking to Herbie and thanking him for his nice printing. And the pages flow out, the type neat and crisp.

In the same way, too, I thank my teeth, I thank my knees, I'm grateful to my hands, I tell my cheekbones how much I like them, and so on. I'm in my seventh decade, and be-bopping along pretty well.

And here's the funny thing—as ugly as my old kitchen was, it was only when I started to try to love it more and care for it more that someone showed up who volunteered to transform it.

SIX

Timing Counts

She was a large woman with tiny feet that barely touched the ground. And even though she was on my table many, many years ago, I will never forget her.

The source of her pain was a father both adored and cruel, a man who had criticized and belittled her throughout her childhood in the 1930s.

As she spoke of him, there was a flash and a picture in my mind of a man in a pair of tweed pants and what looked like the old-fashioned sleeveless one-piece underwear called a union suit. There were also union suits that were more like long underwear, but this was the summer model. "That's it!" she cried, "He always wore that!" Tears filled her eyes, the hurt and the pain roiling at the edge of her skin, as I invited her to begin to release, very gently, a safe amount of that energy.

Suddenly, it seemed that the situation urgently needed some essential rose oil, which carries the vibration of love. I didn't want to leave the table, but excused myself and went to my little supply closet area.

The energy back there was sputtering like a match or firecrackers that just popped and left the crackling sensation of broken air behind them.

A man's gruff voice crackled, too, in my mind. "Give her the gelt!" it demanded. "Give her the GELT!" The insistence and frustration were palpable. I just wasn't sure of the message. There was a mental flash of that union suit. Yes, it was him.

Confused, I began to look on my supply shelf, nestled between rows of books. There were essential oils, candles, matches, incense and sages, flower remedies for topical use, charcoal and resins for the really tough jobs, a little blue ceramic elephant incense holder, a cedarwood box in the shape of a heart . . . and a little net bag of gold foil-covered chocolate coins I had put there in late December for no particular reason other than that I was guided to. That was at least three months earlier. "Coins of the World," the label said, aka Hanukkah gelt. You couldn't live in Brooklyn without knowing that.

As I picked up the little bag, the frustration and anger in the air reduced to a simmer. This guy was definitely some piece of work.

Returning to the table, bag of coins in hand, I said, "This is going to sound weird, but I think your father really wants you to have this," and gently placed the coins in her palm.

Her fingers curled, and her eyes widened. "Hanukkah gelt!" she cried. "Oh, my God! That was the only present my father ever gave me!"

She began to weep softly again, but this time, I felt her heart open like a rose, and the sorrow and suffering began to melt away.

An old Jewish proverb says that the greatest wisdom is kindness.

I say that it's easier to clean up your messes when you're still in a body.

SEVEN

In the Middle of a Phone Call

9/11: How that seamless, cloudless sky cracked open, tore apart wide. In collecting our son from his school on Henry Street that morning, I, along with some kind neighbors, encountered a whirlwind of acrid debris flying low to the ground near the Brooklyn–Queens Expressway, the BQE. Squinting and coughing, we pushed against a blizzard of tiny bits of paper, sheetrock, plastics, and . . . what else?

For weeks afterward, we found paperwork from the desks and files of the World Trade Center in the streets and gutters of Brooklyn. In a pile of mud, I saw a wine inventory list from Windows on the World. Onto my own front stoop flew a page on the topic of risk management, marked Confidential.

But that was not all that swirled in with the plume. In a matter of days, a young, talented Reiki student called me, distraught. The spirits of friends she had worked with at the World Trade Center were all hanging out at her apartment, and her boyfriend was getting fed up. I understood.

In my half-dreams in the restless nights of those days, I would see people hiding in my garage, some with their hands in front of their faces. I invited them into the house. Some refused. When I rode the R train through the ruins of the Cortlandt Street station, a young blonde woman apparently only I could see leaped from the platform into the moving train and sat down next to me. I invited her to come back to my house. She said that there were people on the platform who didn't understand why the train never stopped. I said they could come, too.

My young Reiki student came over with all her friends in spirit, twenty or more. I could sense laughing and joking and chatting among them. My student and I tried to convince them that things would work out better if they went to the Other Side, rather than staying on Earth, where, in time, they might find themselves off the grid and risk becoming wandering spirits or ghosts.

They were amused at her pitch for the hereafter, my green-kerchiefed young friend, for whom, by her own admission, "party" was more a verb than a noun. They were just hitting their stride in life. Some of them had been taken in the middle of a phone call.

But we persisted. I drew an oval in the air, intending it to be a portal to the Beyond. The first one in line, a young, handsome man with obvious leadership qualities, decided to face the unknown. I heard a male voice say something like "Abba Gaba," which I did not understand. The sound was faint, but I physically heard it, which was quite unusual for me.

Then he leaped into the other dimension, and his friends all followed, as if jumping into the inky waters of a star-speckled pond in the wee hours of Prom Night. The young blonde woman from the subway went, as did people from the platform and the garage. We assisted people over until we were tired. They kept flocking in from parts unknown.

"The first guy said something like, 'Abba Gaba,'" I told my student.

She corrected me matter-of-factly. "It's 'Alba gu bràth.' Did you ever see the film *Braveheart*? That's the battle cry. We blasted it on the speakers every morning before we started work."

And as we stood there, we felt the room melt into a sense of peace at last and softly shimmer with light.

EIGHT

Generous Nature

An uncle had a deep enmity against people of color. His angry threats of what he would do if certain people ever crossed his path were shocking. We still don't know for sure what caused it. We were just kids in lily-white schools, unaware of the privilege we carried with us constantly. And stupid and ignorant ourselves, but not homicidal.

Right then, Uncle wasn't doing as well as his brothers. At the kitchen sink, there was a cold-water hand pump instead of faucets. Deep in the side yard, covered in morning-glory vines, was a weathered wooden outhouse in daily use. Sometimes, the pressure in Uncle's little starter home was so great, we children would simply flee into the backyard, the screen door banging, which made him even angrier. We breathed in the sweet-grassy fragrance of a rural Indiana summer with a faint undertone of the outhouse. Heard the chattering birdsong. Walked past my aunt's abundant vegetable garden with its delicate pink pea blossoms shining against the dark earth.

And we went right to the radiant gray tracks of the railroad train that ran directly behind the property. We would put pennies on the tracks, sacrificing them at a time when a penny would buy a large pretzel rod or a jawbreaker. Then we would run back into the yard and wait. After the explosion of sound and steel as the train roared through, we would go and marvel at the smooth copper ovals the pressure of the wheels had left behind, and think gruesome thoughts of what would have happened if we had gotten our fingers caught instead. We wondered how close we'd have to be to get sucked under.

What I didn't realize at the time is that my uncle's hatred of the Other might be because our cultures were so much alike. The poet Charles J. Butler once told me that traditional rural white culture and traditional urban black culture are quite similar.

Today, every time I dress up to attend one of the dos of my friend and fellow Reiki Master Nettie Paisley, an Interfaith Minister and an ethicist who should also be at least the Baroness of Bed-Stuy, I feel enfolded in the sense of occasion that permeated my family's holidays in a golden time before women wore pedal pushers to funerals.

At Nettie's dos, the gentlemen wear suits and ties or turtlenecks and jackets. The ladies also dress beautifully, with glamor and glitter. Nettie offers warm, elegant Southern hospitality trimmed in gilt-edge china so delicate you can see shadows of your fingers through the cup. The music is different, though, and more inspiring. Brooklyn jazz from a lifelong jazz genius like Nettie's husband, Ed Stoute, beats out Patti Page's 78's.

But I have wandered off somewhere.

My poor, angry uncle aged, became a diabetic, suffered with his feet, inspired his wife finally to leave him, and went blind.

The man who came to his house to teach him Braille was—a man of color. I don't know the details except that, reportedly, they got along, and my uncle was grateful for the teaching and the company. That was until the inevitable day came, when someone said:

"You know that man that's coming to your house anymore? Well. . . ."

The next time the Braille teacher showed up, my uncle ordered him out of the house.

Not long after that, Uncle died.

How artful, kind, and compassionate the universe can be: "You may be lame, blind, halt, but we will still give you another chance. We will send a man to teach, help, connect, and guide. You will be able to get to know him, and then you can decide."

What beauty there is in this . . . these strange and poetic opportunities! They arrive almost every day.

We are all truly blessed. We just have to see our own blessings.

NINE

Give It All You've Got, Then Give It Over

When we moved into our frame house in Park Slope, there were eight-year-old yellow–gray tabloid newspapers in the silverware drawers and saucer-sized pink roses in the garden.

The lady of the house and her grown-up son had drawn their battle lines. She stayed out-of-doors; he fried his own breakfast sausage along with a steaming side of resentment. The walls were caked with grease; I used Lestoil on a door that magically transformed from brown to cream.

The house had suffered. When we first arrived, every tap in the house ran constantly. In storms, rainwater cascaded into the granite basement. Somebody said to have the granite basement block repointed, and it helped, but there were still bad leaks, especially in the corner with the circuit breaker box.

We didn't know anything about taking care of houses. I had grown up with a Superdad who owned a tool rental service. My husband had grown up in apartments. Anything wrong was remedied by calling the Super. Superdad, Super—we were clueless.

During that first winter, a mixture of snow, slush, and sidewalk salt slithered underground and knocked out our power. Con Ed temporarily restored electricity by opening the circuit breaker box and hooking us up to a street lamp. The metal doors of the box were wide open, and all the switches were exposed. We were told not to touch it under any circumstance. It was Sunday. On Monday, another terrible storm was due to arrive— this time, with a massive amount of rain. I could imagine the water pouring in over the circuits—the box was ancient. It was a brand with a terrible reputation for fires. We had had no budget to replace it.

I called Con Ed, explained the situation, including my fears, and they said no one could come to make the repairs and close up the box until at least Tuesday. Sorry.

There was a great hardware store nearby run by Italian brothers—Joseph, Peter, and the rest. I threw myself on their mercy and wisdom as if they were the

Franciscans of home repair. They told me that the foundation might be cracked, and I could fortify the foundation outside by looking for cracks and mixing up some powdered stuff to the consistency of pancake batter and stuffing it in. So, I began as a light rain started to fall. I put this stuff into every place I saw a crack. Then, I figured out what part of the foundation corresponded to the circuit breaker box inside, and, for additional protection, I covered that over with heavy-duty plastic held in place by bricks.

And then, I prayed. A lot. "Please help," is basically what I said. "You know my situation. I've done everything I can. Please help." And I let go as much as I could.

The rain was light, yet steady. There was a slowly widening dark streak behind the box, but nothing pouring over. At 2:00 A.M., I gave up, exhausted, and lay down to sleep on the living room sofa. At 4:00 A.M., I heard the door buzzer. Loud and long.

"Cowwn Ed!" a voice cut through the darkness with a South Brooklyn ring. Were there two more beautiful words in the English language? Not on that day. Joyously I let them right in, offered coffee (which they declined), watched them fix the electrical situation and close the box. Only then did I say, "I'm so glad you got here. I thought you guys weren't coming till Tuesday. That's what they told me on the phone."

The guy with the wire cutters had an inscrutable look. "Gosh, I don't know." he said lightly. "Must have been a paperwork mix-up." Outside, it was just starting to storm.

TEN

There Can Be Refuge

In 1978, I took a course in intuitive development and healing in a beautiful Eastern Orthodox Church in New Jersey. The church's golden dome shone like an exotic egg. It was nestled at the bottom of steep hills and, like the headgear of the priests, somehow symbolic of holy seed. In the Eastern Orthodox tradition, Jesus was born in a cave, not a manger.

The sanctuary was painted by the congregants. Each would first kneel in front of the altar, a soft brush laced through entwined fingers, and pray. The colors were vivid and clear—bold images of the Blessed Mother and of Jesus and little traceries of olive leaves that embraced the walls. It was so different from one of the proudly plain churches of my childhood—beige metal folding chairs on a speckled, beige vinyl tile floor, clear picture windows, one American flag, one Sunday school flag, one very bare cross.

In the church in New Jersey, the teacher of intuitive healing was a priest, Father Al, so beloved in the community that everyone took his course—the mayor's wife, college professors and students from the nearby university, accountants, creative folk, people from all walks of life. They sat together: sweater sets and classic bobs, brown leather pants and high boots, chunky gold jewelry and big hair.

This course was designed to teach us, step by step, greater powers of intuition so we could ultimately pick up on medical problems and provide healing long-distance to people we had never met, people for whom we might have little more than a name, an age, and a town. It had been developed by a man who wanted everyone to be able to work, to the best of their abilities, like the great American intuitive Edgar Cayce.

In one of the first exercises, as we listened to the guided meditation, we were mentally to go home and look at our own house from all angles, inside and out, even viewing the upper levels from the outside. One person observed that his shutters had been hung upside down. Another got the impression that his wife was with another man. Both turned out to be true.

The abilities we were learning could be useful in many situations. We discovered this one Saturday in class when a sudden storm coated the hills with ice, including the steepest hill, the one we had to take to the avenue. Class was closed early. We were instructed to drive up this terrible hill, one by one.

With my hands on my chilly steering wheel down in the church parking lot, I looked up and saw Father Al at the top of the hill, standing out in the wind like a young Lear, dark eyes flashing. He turned his head and focused on each car very carefully. At the worst place on the hill, I would see the cars suddenly get traction and move up as if pushed. When it was my turn, I felt it, too—as if my back tires had suddenly bitten into sheer ice. That couldn't be so. Yet, I was safely on the road.

One day near the end of this course, we listened to a guided meditation on creating and outfitting an imaginary laboratory where we could help people heal.

After that, we heard another meditation wherein we would each mentally meet two guides who would come to our imaginary labs to help us—one male, one female.

As the meditation continued, my male guide walked into my lab. He had long, curly hair—given the period, likely a wig—and was dressed in a three-quarter-length coat, pants that stopped at the knees, white stockings, and chunky leather shoes. The metal buttons on his coat cuffs gleamed. I asked his name. He said he was Antonie van Leeuwenhoek.

(I was pleased to get a celebrity scientist. But he did not look like the drawing in the "Annals of Optometry" poster in my eye doctor's office. There, Antonie had soft, reddish-brown hair. Here, his hair or wig was night black. In fact, I later found he more resembled Antonie's one-time employer, Sir William Davidson of Curriehill, a spy for the English crown! I may never have the answer.)

It was time for the female guide to arrive. Her footfall was soft, her moccasins beautiful. She was dressed in fringed white deerskin dotted with sparkling beads, and she carried a basket. I asked her name. She said, "Red Feather." She told me she was a healer who knew about herbs. It seemed to me that she provided a good balance to Antonie.

When the lights were turned back up, Father Al asked us how it had gone. It was all fine. Everyone got their two guides. One person got an extraterrestrial as a guide, but other than that, it was all pretty normal.

Then Father Al told us about a recent class in which something happened that had never happened before.

When he turned up the lights in that class, he said, nearly everyone reported that along with their two guides, their laboratories were filling up with people they didn't know. It didn't make sense to anybody, but the next meditation was to help people who came to their labs. So they did it.

It turned out that just as the students were creating their laboratories and meeting their guides, there was a multicar pileup near the intersection of two highways about half a mile away. The poor visibility that precipitated the accident made it tough for emergency vehicles to arrive quickly.

Father Al's theory was this: the people who flooded the imaginary labs were the injured unconsciously seeking help. Somehow, some part of them found these healing spaces where they could be sustained until physical help came to them.

We will never know for sure. But Father Al had gotten us up the hill. We had reason to believe.

ELEVEN

The Karmic Energy Commission Newsletter

When the 1980s rolled in, one segment of the "New Age Movement" focused on money and manifestation. If we could visualize and manifest precisely what we wanted, we considered ourselves pretty far along.

It never occurred to us that this resonated with the Puritan belief that if someone had more cattle than someone else, God must be smiling on them. We didn't see that mentally and energetically hammering away at a situation to appease our conscious desires might not always be the best path. At that time, I thought of my body as a briefcase for my brains. It took a while for me to learn that my conscious mind is a set of buttons on my multidimensional shirt. Nice buttons, and useful ones—but buttons.

At that time, my family and I were a bit cool toward each other after I had ended a marriage of two and a half years. My old friends had bid me adieu without explaining why. My coworkers in advertising were bewildered, then outraged, at my combination of sweetness and backbiting. I was drinking too much wine at parties, working long hours, and very lonely.

It was then that I discovered a couple I'll call Mr. and Mrs. Wallet. They spoke about God and prosperity and breathing. Mr. Wallet's own handsome billfold was thick with Bens, which he showed off proudly. They had a big following. In retrospect, I imagine that many of their students had an interest in spiritual topics and a slightly threadbare relationship with their own families. The Wallets could be our new, youngish, hip teachers/ parents/friends. They hugged us. They gave lots of parties. They were glad to see us at every seminar.

And the seminars were truly helpful. But in time, the joy of knowing the Wallets wore thin. There were rumors of a special relationship with a student on the Mister's part—an emotional affair. When I assisted in their seminar on God, I discovered that Mr. and Mrs. Wallet were not drinking ice water during class as we were asked to do. Their oversized balloon goblets perched near the blackboard were filled with chilled white wine. They smoked pot on the breaks in their hotel room. And I watched the Wallets become furious with the waitstaff at the hotel dining room when a rebellious student slyly took one of the better tables.

Not long after that, Mr. Wallet had an angry confrontation with me because I was not going to do a particular long-term course with him on the nature of love. The cost was five thousand dollars; we exchanged nothing but words. As I walked down the stoop of his Manhattan apartment, my nose began to bleed profusely and I fished for a crumpled, damp tissue in my purse.

Twenty years later, I met the old man on whose teachings Mr. Wallet had based his work. Dressed in a silken, cream-colored Nehru suit and pointed, shining slippers, this man was so old, he told the assembled group, that he had been senile but aged out of it. And he laughed.

There was a moment on a break when the air and time both stood still, and there was no one else around this man but me. It was as if we were in a bubble. I told him of my experience with the Wallets two decades earlier. He looked me in the eyes—his were still very clear, and somehow reflected sunlight on the Himalayas—and apologized for their behavior. He said that their operation had been shut down. I was far from the only one to have complained.

I must confess that this information was strangely satisfying. Yet part of me wanted to say, "And can I have my money back, those thousands of dollars?" But of course I knew better.

For the Wallets had been my perfect mirrors. They sold stuff for money, and so did I. Their relationships were highly conditional, and so were mine. They wanted precisely what they wanted when they wanted it, and energetically worked to move heaven and earth to get it. And I had been happy to learn from them.

I had disrespected the very nature of love by assuming that it could be bought for the price of a seminar. Or, that it could be mine if I visualized really hard and was very specific.

Truly, water seeks its level. (Wine probably does, too.) Thank you, Mr. and Mrs. Wallet, for everything you taught me. Because of you. And in spite of you. I got it all. Bless you.

It was later in my work that I learned the path of "letting" rather than "insisting." Diane Stein, a pioneer in modern Reiki, said not to specify the name or face of a desired lover, but rather to imagine the feel of a kiss or the touch of a hand in a joyful, fulfilling relationship.

Not to mention that precise phrasing for our wishes can raise problems. I heard years ago of a widow who kept praying for "a man in the house." She came home one day and surprised a burglar. When I was going to do my first Reiki for a Fortune 500 company, I was nervous and asked repeatedly for a safe place to work. When I got there, I was given a tiny storage room full of files and a giant green safe. A safe place. Was the universe saucy, kind, or literal?

It became more and more clear that the ethical thing to do about a situation is to ask above all for the Best Possible Outcome and the Highest Good for all concerned. To intend that. To ask to be guided as to my part in the proceedings. To do that part. And to know when to let go.

This idea of asking for the Best Possible Outcome and the Highest Good for all concerned is a powerful one. It is the intention that allows a situation to turn out more elegantly than our conscious minds could imagine. And it helps us from having karmic messiness on our hands.

And so, when a bright young student comes to study Reiki One and tells me proudly that she can melt a cloud with her mind and control the weather, I find myself flicking invisible ash off an imaginary bubblegum cigarette—in a hypothetical holder longer even than Audrey Hepburn's in *Breakfast at Tiffany's*.

And I say, with the requisite languor and a froggy touch of Bette Davis, "That's all well and good—very nice, indeed. But that's not quite the point of it." And then I explain.

TWELVE

Animals Get It

Three Reiki practitioners, myself included, went to a cat shelter one day to offer energy healing. Cats typically have large territories they like to defend from other cats. So, despite the kindness of organizations who take them in, put a roof over their little furry heads, feed and care for them, and of course, save them from dying, some situations are of necessity less than ideal. This one was—dozens of cats in a space the size of a one-bedroom apartment.

The aroma was equally intense—it was a shrill smell of cat urine, urine, urine, like a constant, blaring siren. As we picked our way in and a smiling attendant swabbed the broken but clean vinyl tile floors, we noticed a tiny cat-sized recamier lounge and a dainty little fountain with a lion's head where the cats could drink. Had these come from a dotty benefactor? Cats threaded among each other—it was like an eternal 8:35 A.M. in the main concourse of Grand Central. There were also "bad cats" in cages—they couldn't walk around because they were a danger to others. Hand-lettered cardboard signs taped to the bars warned us to keep fingers out.

Every group creates its own energy field, and we wanted to make this one more peaceful. We started by improving the general energy, air-writing Reiki symbols in each corner of the space, and letting the soothing energy pour through our fingers out into the room.

We found ourselves drawn to the energetic "hot spots," mostly the "bad cats," first. They turned their backs and ignored us. But some shuddered gently, which was their trauma releasing. We worked on pinked ears and missing eyes; we worked from our hearts and on theirs.

This was followed by the "sad cats," including one green-eyed, long-haired white female who indicated to us that she feared she would never, ever be adopted. Several people had seen her, but no one had taken her home. Two of the Reiki practitioners were also professional makeup artists. They told her precisely what to do: fluff up when people arrive to look at you. Look cute rather than dejected. If she did that, we sensed she would be adopted soon, and we indicated that to her. Her posture changed, her eyes began to sparkle, and she started grooming her coat.

At this point, we stopped for a moment, because there was a weird banging in the room. We found it was coming from a cage we hadn't noticed before—a little clutch of brown rabbits, undoubtedly secured for their own safety. One of them had picked up a metal dish full of rabbit kibble with his mouth and was banging it against the bars. Kibble hit the floor. We looked at them. "Do YOU want Reiki?" We started to offer it to them. We could feel them drawing it in immediately. And then we realized: these rabbits were imprisoned on an alien cat planet. They needed all the help they could get. One tilted back his head as he received the energy, and did a "Fuf-fuf-fuf-fuf-fuf" with his muzzle. Their little chests rose and fell as they all began to breathe more deeply.

Who had the better time that day, the little four-leggeds, or us?

Often attributed to Chief Seattle, but actually written for his character in a film, are the following words: "What is man without the beasts? If all the beasts were gone, man would die from great loneliness of spirit, for whatever happens to the beasts also happens to man. All things are connected." Indeed. Indeed. Indeed.

THIRTEEN

Go for the Cheeseburger

This was inspired by a story from July 2006 in the Naples, Florida, *Daily News*. My mother clipped and sent it to me. She has been wonderfully supportive of my Reiki work, and I am grateful for her encouragement. Not every Mom would be willing to give up the reflected glory of some of the big corporate names in advertising—the round holes into which my rhomboid peg had tried to fit itself again and again (the very definition of insanity). To everyone I ever worked with in nearly thirty years in the ad game, thank you for your patience. And thanks to Mom!

In Naples, there is a private animal center called the Shy Wolf Sanctuary. I visited it a few years ago, and offered Reiki energy to all the animals who wanted it. It was touching to see them press themselves up against the fences, the chain links making diamond patterns in their fur, as they came as close as possible to my hands.

Shy Wolf was home to misfits and rarities, a few resembling something out of a surreal animated sixties cartoon by Chuck Jones. There were Omega wolves—just the opposite of Alpha wolves. There were wolf-dogs. There was even a cross-bred big cat with the proportions of a coffee table.

Amazingly, there was also a Florida panther. As he coolly appraised me with glimmering golden eyes, I started to shiver. Years earlier, when the species was all but extinct, I had written an ad for a Florida panther sculpture. Now, before me was a mythical animal—or nearly so—resting in the sun atop a wooden box within a small, graveled enclosure. I offered him Reiki energy. From all indications, he refused it. I tried again and then moved on.

But, to the *Daily News* story that Mom sent me later: an abused wolf-dog had been brought to the Shy Wolf Sanctuary. His neck skin was lapping over a collar so tight he could barely breathe. After the collar was removed, he was given proper veterinary care. But he refused to eat. The people caring for him tried dog food. No response. Then they tried wolf food—mostly organ meat, if I recall. Nothing. Not a bite. Finally, they brought in a gifted animal communicator. The wolf-dog indicated to her that he wanted a cheeseburger on a china plate, just like in a restaurant. They went into the house and made one. Cheese, meat, and a bun, and they put it on a plate. Probably no lettuce or tomato.

The wolf-dog immediately ate half the burger and buried the other other half for a midnight snack, as the article said. After that, he would eat whatever they provided.

To me, the question in his heart was, "Can I trust you? Will you truly care for me?" And he gave them a very special test. They listened to him, and they passed.

In the golden web of life—as opposed to the Golden Arches—we are all responsible for our own cheeseburgers. But there are times when each of us needs to know that someone will listen to the call of our heart, as wild, peculiar, and unreasonable as it might be. Just to listen without judgment or correction.

Noble wolf, thank you for that teaching. What can I bring you?

FOURTEEN

We're Not Nearly Alone

There's a point in every child's life when the Santa Claus story has been dusted off one too many times. At age six, I distinctly remember whining at my mother, "If Santa Claus brings us presents, why does my sweater box say 'J.C. Penney?'" She looked at me with a tough-love Mom-ray and said, "Figure it out!" My dear brother and sister can attest to the strength of that ray.

Assuming that we are the universe's only intelligent life is as outdated as thinking that the sun revolves around the Earth.

I saw a former astronaut speak, one who had grown up in the West. He said that the good people of Roswell, New Mexico, loved him as a son of the desert and the stars. When some of them were near to death, they'd called him into their homes and told him that the stories about Roswell and the aliens were absolutely true.

Many years ago, a friend of mine worked at a college radio station, where he interviewed Betty Hill of the famed abduction couple. Once off the air, he asked Betty if she had had further communication with the star beings. She said that she had recently lost a ring— a present from her husband, Barney, who had passed— and wanted it back very much. One night, she said, she came home, and there in the middle of the dining room table, in a pile of dry leaves and dirt, was her ring. It was as if something had sucked up the whole mass and deposited it on the polished wood.

I saw Frank Edwards, the broadcaster and UFOlogist, in 1966. He had been fired from the Mutual Broadcasting System about a decade earlier, at least partly, some believe, because of his many flying saucer stories. Intense, with black-framed glasses, he talked to our group of journalism students about ferreting out the truth. As he spoke, Frank, a year from death, suddenly went into a terrible coughing spasm. "Buy Christmas Seals," he quipped, and went on with his lecture. He was as solid as a sycamore. His book *Flying Saucers: Serious Business* is a classic of the genre.

Nobody has carved a symbolic, spidery glyph in my back garden; no passing craft has blacked out my electric power. I have no physical proof of my own to offer you of any star connections. All I have are impressions—do what you will with them; there are others who can offer you far more. But these are my little possible—I emphasize *possible*—encounters. I will just give you the story, and you can determine for yourself. I'm not 100 percent sure.

In 2002, I felt the presence of some short beings clearly of superior intelligence, and with an unusual energy—higher frequency and more focused than nature spirits, for instance. My brilliant and highly intuitive student described it the same way, too. Yet these folk said to us, upon first meeting, "Why do you go dashing about in boxes on wheels, sometimes bumping into each other?" Feeling tricked, a little fearful and suspicious, I snapped, "This is a disingenuous question!" Well, yes, it was.

Two years later, I was reminded of it when I reread one of my favorite books, *The Magic of Findhorn*. As it relates, in 1966, a distinguished scholar, Robert Ogilvie Crombie, was startled to physically see a little faun—half boy, half animal—in the Edinburgh Royal Botanic Garden. The faun was considerably more shocked to be seen by Robert. One of the first questions the boy-animal asked was precisely the one about the boxes on wheels.

I hit my forehead with the heel of my hand.

Like every other comedian, my small friends knew that if you have to explain a joke, it's no good. Later, I discovered that someone else had worked with beings who answered to the same description—short, great energy workers, and funny. Diane Stein, pioneer of modern Reiki, called them "The Jupiter Comedy and Surgery Team."

Still unsure, one day, in the presence of another student, I said, "If you guys are really who you say you are, can you do something about the floors in this house? Can you make them stronger?" I was seeking information and the potential for home improvement all in one. Just after I said that, my student and I both felt the floor beneath us snap into place, and she commented that it was as if a force had come from beneath it. After that, it did not creak or sag. That still proves nothing, but it certainly showed certain abilities on their part.

Despite their cracking wise, and my initial "I-didn't-just-fall-off-a-turnip-truck" response, we did become connected, and they have done some superb energy work.

But it's not all hearts and flowers and stars. With one client, I kept having very uncomfortable visions. My feet were clearly on the floor in the Reiki room in Brooklyn, my hands were on the Reiki table; yet I would simultaneously see myself looking down at Brazil and the Amazon from a distance so high it was like looking at a globe, although everything I saw was alive. I could see both coasts of South America very clearly, as could my client.

In one vision, I was in the air, then suddenly approaching a partly ruined temple hidden in a jungle. A cracked column rested on the jungle floor. It was possible that this temple did not exist in the present day, or in this dimension. If a normal person walked through the area, I remember thinking, they would never see it.

I found myself in line with a lot of small beings, all of them gray. And somehow, I was gray, too. Or at least I blended in. They each had a small device up one nostril—I did too. It looked and felt like a crescent shape, and it seemed to help their adaptation to the environment.

When we got inside the temple, I saw in the center of a large hall a bearded male human of late middle age. Invisibly restricted to a small area with an ancient ceramic tile floor, he was lurching as if drunk, barely vertical. He seemed to be a very smart man, and they were somehow using him as a Wikipedia. I objected to this practice in the name of humankind and was whisked out of there at once. Never saw them again. No more rides, either.

I know these are nothing more than visions. There are so many books, videos, and films out there—some sensationalist and poorly documented, some deliberate frauds, but some with compelling evidence to consider.

In 2013, astronomers at the Harvard–Smithsonian Center for Astrophysics reported that "six percent of red dwarf stars have habitable, Earth-sized planets. Since red dwarfs are the most common stars in our galaxy, the closest Earth-like planet could be just 13 light-years away." All I'm saying is it's time to give up our terra-centricity. Get over it. Figure it out.

Since we are all citizen-journalists today, I believe the big scoop will come from the streets. My guess is that the first unassailable photo of a star brother or sister to be flashed around the world will be captured by a cell phone and tweeted out, #STARRIFIC!!!!

Now, why am I sensing short beings giving me the interplanetary sign for "meh"?

FIFTEEN

Gang Aft Agley

In the late 1990s, we developed the Brooklyn Email Reiki Chain. Before that, it had been a telephone chain, and if you've ever played "Operator," you can imagine how fragmented the messages became as they passed from answering machine to answering machine.

A group of Reiki practitioners would simultaneously receive an email request and send long-distance Reiki *pro bono* to people who requested it for medical difficulties, and often to entire families and caregivers as well, if asked. A number of happy reports were sent back our way, along with notes of thanks and appreciation.

A standout case for me involved a relative of a relative by marriage. Bradley (name changed) worked in construction. One sizzling summer day, he toppled down two stories. Onto cement. Directly onto his head. Without a helmet.

The email asking for help said that his was the worst case in the Trauma Unit by far. Not expected to live the night. Please send Reiki.

It was delicate, though; if someone is unconscious, one can't ask their permission to send Reiki directly to them. And I was taught it's not ethical to send directly to someone without their permission.

But time was of the essence, so I intuitively asked Bradley's higher self if he wanted Reiki. I got an emphatic "Yes"; but just to make sure, I used a "belt-and-suspenders" approach. I affirmed that if I got it wrong, let the Reiki energy meant for Bradley bless the planet. Ultimately, I gave everything over to God, as always.

Many Reiki practitioners in New York connected energetically with Bradley and sent Reiki. There were also a number of people in his community praying. When Bradley did come back to consciousness, we were encouraged to keep going. Bradley had extra motivation to get stronger faster—he had received custody of his children after a difficult divorce.

I could feel Bradley blaming himself for the fall, for the negligence of not wearing the helmet, for the foolishness of the accident, for what he was putting everyone through. I kept whispering, through space and time, "Things happen, Bradley! Nobody knows why for sure. Quit being hard on yourself and use this energy to get better!"

You can tell when people in a crisis are strongly motivated to heal. The energy began to fly through my hands, which were also often hot. Other people kept sending and praying as well.

From every report, he was sailing through his therapy, even skipping steps. The doctors could not make sense of what was going on. Within two months, Bradley was reapplying for his driver's license. We received a letter of gratitude from his mother. Except for some temporary short-term memory issues, he was expected to do just fine.

The next time I went back to my home town, the relative who had requested help for Bradley sat down at a kitchen table where I was drinking tea, glared at me, and said furiously, "Do you think it's possible that some people are intended to die and should be left to do it? Brad hasn't been the same since the accident. He's angrier than he was."

My jaw dropped. You could have stuffed me with green beans topped with crunchy canned onions and smothered in cream of mushroom soup.

Fortunately, a new addition to the family was trained as a psychologist. She overheard, and interceded with:

"Head trauma like Bradley's very often affects personality. People can get angry far more easily. There's a lot of clinical evidence to support this."

When I got over the shock, I realized that beneath the anger was a heart filled with love and anguish. Had we overstepped our bounds? Was Brad's body healed and his psyche in tatters? Maybe if I had been adding the clearly stated intention of Best Possible Outcome in those days, it would have sweetened the energy and process somehow for Bradley. Who can say?

What have I learned? If you are going to walk the line between life and death, take it from me: you'd better wear sensible shoes.

SIXTEEN

Lively Lessons from the Deceased

One of the first family members in spirit I saw in the Reiki room was somebody's grandmother. She was wearing a bib apron and something white on her head, and so I thought she might have been a nurse from World War I. As it turns out, she was a professional chef at a time when most women were at most good home cooks, and her granddaughter always thought her apron was weird.

I've found that when the dead come back, they show something that clearly identifies them. An uncle modeled his shiny shoes and fanned playing cards in his hand. A grandmother pulled out a tray of Sicilian cookies. Another grandmother opened her hands to reveal rosaries. Someone's Brazilian cousin cooked as I described his ingredients and technique. A grandfather showed his newspaper folded in fourths. These are the calling cards of the dearly departed.

When I saw in my mind's eye a charming middle-aged woman with dark, curly hair, in a trim little suit, she immediately handed me a calendar. My mind went to some baroque idea about the fleeting nature of time.

The client recognized the description immediately: it was her adorable Aunt Tess, who had passed not long ago. She didn't know anything about the calendar, though.

"I get the sense that she dressed with far more taste than money," I said, "She is so well put together, but she doesn't shop at exclusive stores."

"That's Aunt Tess!" the client said, "Everything beautifully coordinated, even though she was always on a budget."

Aunt Tess somehow invited me into her cute kitchen —I still don't know how she did it, but the client agreed that that sounded just like Tess. And then the client asked a question: "When we move to California, what kind of tree does Aunt Tess think we should plant in our yard?"

I heard "Grapefruit!" and relayed it back. "Aunt Tess said we should always eat grapefruit to be beautiful!" the client said with a smile, "She was an Avon Lady."

Well, now I understood the mystery of the calendar. Avon Ladies used to give out calendars as promotional items. It was that simple.

As if she heard me, Aunt Tess turned my way and said, "You're looking a little pale, dear. You could use a nice rosy-pink lipstick. It would bring out your eyes." "Oh, great," I thought. "I've never been much with cosmetics, and now I'm getting makeover tips from the dead."

But she was such a lively, warm being even in her current state that if she'd had a physical lipstick for me, I would have bought it in a heartbeat, and asked for the nail polish to match or coordinate—whatever Aunt Tess thought was best. What she taught me, I guess, is that if you really learn to love life, you'll keep on loving it even after death. Beautiful!

SEVENTEEN

All Time Is Now

Before I write another story, let me say that I believe in angels. Here is what their energy is like for me—loving, yet very reserved, like those cool teacher characters in movies about teenagers in schools in tough neighborhoods in the sixties. An angel is like that teacher who barely dignifies your juvie crap and just keeps loving you through that painful experience of becoming something greater and realer than you were. But it's not all hearts and flowers and it's not gushy. At least not in my experience.

I once offered a workshop called "An Evening with the Angels," which had been chattily well attended in the past. This time, only five people signed up and there the list stayed. "Great," I said, and we did it. In four minutes, my agenda was out the window, as we all sensed and felt major angels coming into the room softly lit by winter candlelight. We described the angels aloud, and our individual visions essentially corroborated each other's, right down to the blisters on Saint Michael's hands. One person mentioned it, and another said, "I saw them, too, but I didn't want to sound pessimistic."

I love the angels. But there are so many beautiful books on angels already, I'd like to tell you about something different in the rest of this, our seventeenth story.

One of my most fascinating experiences was the receiving of a friendly visit one day by a group of French monks from the Middle Ages.

The Middle Ages never impressed me as a fun era; I am put in mind of Saint Teresa of Ávila, who was slogging along in the mud and the rain in an oxcart somewhere just at the end of the Middle Ages. She reportedly looked to the heavens, and said, "Lord, if this is how you treat your friends. . . ."

We got the feeling that whenever and wherever the monks' abbey might have been, there wasn't much to do in the off hours except hole up and try stuff. Perhaps they were quarantined because of the plague. Maybe they couldn't move in space, so they opted for time. But this part is pure speculation; let me continue with what we experienced.

All I know is that there were six or seven monks led by a thirty-something-year-old with curly dark hair. When they landed in my Reiki room, I was doing a session with a student who is amazingly intuitive. We simultaneously remarked on their presence; they suddenly came in near the window right across from my storage closet. Although we could only see them mentally, the student and I finished each other's sentences in describing them.

These monks seemed to have the joy of the Tim Robbins character in *The Shawshank Redemption* when he's finally free.

I told them mentally that it was the year of Our Lord 2008, and that the metal boxes with wheels (yes, those again) that they could see through the window were called automobiles. I told them what cars did and how they worked. I mentioned that we were definitely women, in case they were confused by our clothing, and it was now permissible—at least for some of us—to go without head coverings and to wear pants.

We got the feeling that the only thing that made sense to them in the entire room was the candle burning.

So we thought we'd give them some good stories to take back and whisper after vespers. We showed them the black torchère floor lamp and what happened when we moved the dimmer switch. We put a CD in the boom box and began to play it. I think we played something classical. I wish we had also played Elvis. Or Edith Piaf. Wouldn't that have been fun?

I sang "Gaudeamus Igitur," the classic university song in Latin. Everyone knows the instrumental, but few people know the words. Two years of *amo/amas/amat* in high school finally paid off big time. They loved it. Blessed mother tongue.

We pulled some of the books out of my closet, showed them the photographs within, and let them see how plentiful books were, since they could be printed. We even showed them a small book with photos of Irish illuminated manuscripts, just to let them know that we knew that monks did this stuff—that it was still admired today.

There was so much more we could have done, but remember, we were in the middle of someone's session. Come to think of it, the monks probably would have loved the bathroom plumbing, but we stayed in the Reiki room. No sense totally flipping them out.

The leader just smiled and smiled as he looked around, the light pouring through his curls.

The team came back just once more, but that was the last of it. Perhaps the abbot got wind of their activities and sent them out to grow peas. I guess an abbey at that time would be a lot like a small town in the Midwest: "You don't see much here, but what you hear makes up for it."

So, if you ever find yourself in France, looking at illuminated manuscripts in some illustrious museum, and you see a lovely border of vines entwining themselves around the page, and you look a little closer, and just behind the vines you think—how weird!—that you see a black Crate and Barrel torchère floor lamp, you could be absolutely right.

And you will know something important about that beautiful book: the people who made it—made it to Brooklyn.

EIGHTEEN

Past Tense

In the Reiki room, some of the personal issues we deal with appear to have been hundreds of years in the making. Clients experience what are generally called "past lives," the idea of having lived with the same soul or essence, in a different body, with a different identity, during a time that seems to precede our own.

But there are experts who also say that all of our lives, including past and future, are happening simultaneously. Wrapping one's mind around the implications of that idea is similar to visiting Bloomingdale's in the 1980s, when every potential path to the exits was blocked either by a charmingly aggressive spritz jockey with linebacker-sized, silk-jacketed shoulders, or by a full-length mirror, mysteriously looming and floating in some dramatic half-light.

Dr. Hank Wesselman, a respected anthropologist who had worked alongside the Leakeys in East Africa, began in the 1970s to have visions of a life that belonged to him some five thousand years in the future, and wrote several autobiographical books on the topic. The future Hank is a member of a hunter-gatherer society who makes his way through the quiet, verdant world and rusted ruins of the once-great cities on the North American continent. There are times when this future-life person sees his own visions of a peculiar past life, that being Hank's world, including its cars, paved roads, dishwashers, and other phenomena that might look puzzling to someone trekking across a tangled landscape with an iron-tipped spear.

Dr. Wesselman taught that there are levels of reality. In everyday reality, everything is separate, there are beginnings and endings, a past, present, and future, and cause and effect. Very Newtonian and left-brained. On a higher level of reality, everything is connected, there are only cycles and transitions, all time is now, and the realm of metaphor is quite powerful. Very, let's say, "photonian" and right-brained. Extend this theory, and if you go to a future life, and solve a problem there, it could very positively affect your current life. And vice versa. And versa vice. And by the way, there are also parallel lives, in which a "past life" overlaps another life.

These are separate from parallel dimensions of a present-day life, wherein there is a version of you that did take "the road not taken" and has truly sailed to Fiji, or become a world-class journalist, or had triplets, or finally learned to ice skate.

A practical application of this, stemming from a useful concept in energy work, is that there is at least one alternate dimension of you already doing the very thing you want (and perhaps fear) to do. Therefore, you can ask for the energy, information, and resources from that other dimension—make a copy of it—and bring it into your own dimension and into your heart chakra to help you achieve the thing that feels like a more authentic expression of you. Now, if you were listen to Bashar, purportedly a future and extraterrestrial self of Darryl Anka, channeled by him in this life, you would hear that you aren't changing yourself, you are merely jumping to a parallel reality.

Oh, my stars and garters! I used to tell people, "You're just the tip of your own iceberg." Of course, I don't use that expression anymore. Nevertheless, there's a lot of you that you don't even know exists. It's like herding cats—Cheshire cats.

Even if you don't believe in reincarnation, an alternative life vision might be a powerful metaphor for a current problem, and might create a way to heal that problem's effects without revealing its most tenderly threatening parts.

I've worked mostly with past lives, and in so doing have found myself in an ancient Egyptian embalming room wherein I could physically smell the cinnamon, cedar, and myrrh; a sand-swept Mongolian yurt; a sewing studio serving chubby French nobility; an eighteenth-century Austrian ball; a Chinese artisan's market reduced to splinters by horsemen bandits. I've also been witness to many simpler lives that had their own dreams and dramas of love and grief.

There have been a number of stories of wars and insurrections, from the Crusades through Vietnam. The negative and traumatic, sadly, makes a more vivid, easily accessible energetic impression than the beautiful and serene. One woman currently from East Asia described in remarkable detail the everyday life and emotional state of a soldier in what I pieced together as possibly the Crimean War. When I later showed her the photographs online, she was flabbergasted. She had even described being a "grunt" at an investigation on the conduct of the war, and research revealed that there were indeed investigations, resulting from what were considered to be mismanaged land campaigns.

How can one deal with issues that emerge in past lives? Here are three possibilities: simply to observe, to choose to change the past, or to change something in the present.

To observe is just to take away the lesson of the life: what worked, and what could have been done better? I have attended workshops with people who say, in essence, learn from the life and close the book. I say, learn from the life, but the book is still open. It is always open.

To alter the past is to take an action within the vision of that life: go back into the life you've just seen and feed the hungry whom you allowed to suffer; help the families of the men you lost in battle; get to the radio room in time to save the fleet; refuse to cheat your mother out of her pension; quit overworking your indentured servant; look out for the small boy heading toward the water. Make things right.

To change effectively in the present is to take the lesson of the past and to do things differently now. If you, say, were responsible for tearing up a Chinese artisans' market long, long ago, you could help some artisans now. (Come to Brooklyn! They're everywhere!) You could make a donation to a Chinese Benevolent Association. Assuming you still liked to ride horses, you could even volunteer to teach kids how to ride responsibly. Or, you could consider and change where you still might be riding roughshod over your loved ones' lives. If those "all time is now" theories are correct, your present-day actions will positively affect the past and the future.

I have had my own adventures running my stick through the spokes of time. On a ballroom floor in a Mexican hotel in about 1984, I went into a meditation, and suddenly up sprang a past life from the late 900s in Europe. I caught a brief glimpse of the Danube. Apparently, my life's goal then had been to create peace among warring tribes and factions throughout the area.

But instead, at the first major provocation, I felt my biceps flex as I picked up a mace, a potentially lethal metal ball on a stick. It felt familiar. I knew I could use it well. And I went to work bashing in heads. As I watched this carnage, my present-life self began to wail in a way that I have not done before or since—not for the death of President Kennedy when I was a tween— not for anyone I have loved in this life. This pain came from the gut of my soul.

One of the seminar leaders came over, and through my tears I saw a perfectly pedicured foot, the toes blinking a luminescent pink, and a pretty leather sandal with a beaten coppery heel. At first, the person was sympathetic and tried to calm me, but then pronounced me a drama queen, and went on. I didn't care. I had never seen this in myself and knew that it was important to let it roll. Oddly enough, one of my most frequent comments to my coworkers to that date had been, "Hey, I don't mean to hit you over the head with this, but. . . ."

As the years rolled by, I learned to stop fighting and start helping people in distress in settings ranging from the New York medical examiner's office after 9/11, to various shelters and aid centers after Hurricane Sandy. I have also made several initiatives specifically to help military veterans. No biggie—and I can still do more. But it was, you see, a step in the right direction.

One evening in 2010, I was attending a community meeting where the topic was aircraft noise over Brooklyn. There were representatives from the FAA and Port Authority on one side of the table; in opposition were neighborhood groups able to document decibels with a precision and thoroughness that was scary. In addition to showing their data, one group shared a letter from an individual who believed that the noise level was exacerbating her cancer.

The representatives of the FAA said that they had been using the same flight patterns for many years, and that those routes maximized safety, and that was that. The room was filled with tension and the feeling that never would these two sides come to terms.

Aha. I knew from my past work in advertising that, for a shockingly long time, air traffic controllers had been keeping planes unsnarled with technology from the 1970s. Only in recent years were new equipment and systems being introduced. I prayed silently and spoke aloud.

I started by praising, from my heart, what air traffic controllers had done with Pong-era equipment for so long, stating that if everybody here knew what the controllers had been up against technologically, they would likely be grateful. And then I suggested that somehow, maybe, as state-of-the-art equipment was being rolled out, and controllers could benefit from its precision, the tolerances of the air routes could be revisited.

Such a silly little comment. But for me, just after, there was a kind of silvery silence at the end of the table where the two sides sat. The energy flowed in the air like a plane circling to land, or a flail—a metal ball on a chain considered an advance over maces—whirling but ceasing to make its mark. And then, the meeting leader made a large clockwise circle with his hand to encompass both the FAA representatives and the scarily scientific neighbors, and said, "Now, all of you are on the same committee. You will work on this situation together to solve it."

That meeting leader soon left for the Far East with his family, and I don't think his request ever got off the ground. Nevertheless, the door that opened a little that night for me also seemed to let the Mace Wielder pass through—once he dropped his weapon.

NINETEEN

Break It Up

When we moved into our very old new house, a Reiki friend of mine came over to clear it energetically. She found a ghost of a small, shy boy named Donnie in the pantry. Months later, an elderly neighbor confirmed that sweet child's name and his early demise.

In time, I began to do this kind of work, too, but the places I visited seemed entrenched in difficult energy. (Yes, yes, I know, like attracts like.)

Rupert Sheldrake, the British biochemist and parapsychologist, stated, more or less, that a space that has habitually experienced a certain kind of activity will begin to support that activity. In practical terms, this means that if you often fight in the bedroom, the bedroom will start to be the place that encourages fighting. That's the energy field being built.

Not only that, but it's my experience that the energy of each space is highly readable, even by people who don't know they are reading it. Nearly everyone has walked into a place and said, "Ugh, I don't know what it is, but I don't want to stay here." That's likely to be energy talking to you.

Often, I clear apartments before new people move in. In one place, pure rage was simmering in the stale air of an empty, echoing kitchen. Later I learned that the prior tenants, a couple, had stopped furiously chopping vegetables one night and started a knife fight with each other.

Sometimes, a home suddenly and mysteriously starts troubling its owners. More than once, I have walked in and made a beeline for a piece of art recently purchased on holiday. The emanated energy is so dark and dreadful that when it is cleared, even the physical light in the room visibly improves. Domestic artists can also create problematic paintings. What comes to mind is a wintry woodland scene radiating a depression so deep, I could feel it across the East River.

One condo I visited had previously been a notorious bachelor pad. The amount of energy in the bathrooms was crazy. As I started on the ladder up to the roof, I got clear visions of topless women mashing their breasts onto the skylight over the living room, and a lot of drinking on the roof, with empty bottles of top-shelf liquor being thrown in every direction.

"Ugh," I thought, "You're getting totally carried away." But as I emerged through the hatch and stood on the roof, a quick visual survey showed that there were indeed sparkling glass booze bottles—some smashed—resting on the roofs of all the neighboring homes in a full 360, the sun glinting off their faces. As for the women, we will never know. After I worked on the roof, breaking up old energy with a rattle, the owner of the home told me that her very large cat, who hadn't been feeling well, began to purr with contentment and delight.

Some people will ask me, "Well, I burn sage in my house. Isn't that enough?" Not always. Mother Sage is a powerful purifier. But many homes have layer upon layer of energetic information within their walls, and may require a stronger approach.

Here is something you can do for your house, even if you have never studied any kind of energy work. Start by putting together a space-clearing tool kit. Get a box or two of sea salt or kosher salt, and a new broom and dustpan. Find a rattle, or, if that seems awkward to you, make a rattle out of an old mint tin, a few dried beans, and an all-important rubber band. If you have a little set of bells, that's lovely, too. And, of course, get some dried sage, often available at health food stores. Certain resins, burned over charcoal, produce more dramatic results, but they have the distinct disadvantage of smelling a lot like an electrical fire in progress.

On the day you want to do your clearing, make sure the kids are elsewhere. The little ones are sponges for energy. The older ones will be weirded out by your process.

Next, set an intention for the Best Possible Outcome, Highest Good for all concerned. Just state that out loud, and stick to it. Imagine yourself in a protective bubble in the color that pops into your mind.

Start by shaking kosher or sea salt onto the floor of every room where you know it won't be a safety hazard or a problem, leave it there for about ten minutes, then sweep up all the salt and throw it out immediately, Out, out. As in outside in the trash. Next, take your rattle (or mint tin) and go to the room with the dullest, darkest look and feel, and begin to rattle, rattle, rattle, with the intention of breaking up negative energy. Continue until the room—and its colors—look brighter. Repeat this process in all the other rooms.

Next, light some sage, and very carefully, in a large fireproof bowl, with protective gloves if necessary, take the sage from room to room, letting its smoke emanate into every corner. Be very careful of sparks or dropped pieces. You can also try incense if you don't have sage. If they both make you nervous from a fire perspective, take some pretty little bells or gongs, and ring them in the rooms instead. Or, go in and gently sing, "Ahhhhhhh!" on an F or F-sharp. That's a heart sound.

Finally, tackle the disorganization in each room, especially the closets. Energy affects matter, which then affects energy, which affects matter. Closets can be negative energy magnets for several reasons: you may have some real "energy bombs" among the items hidden away. How about the jacket from that person you discovered cheating on you? Or, you may open the closet every day, and get annoyed—you can't find your stuff, you don't like what you see—and you cast that energy on the contents of the closet. Plus, dark energy loves overstuffed, messy nooks and crannies. (Mice do, too!)

Of course I have busted my share of ghosts. I have found lascivious old spirits lurking in more than one young woman's shower stall; a low-level Tammany Hall type of spirit (who apparently sold stock in some Brooklyn railroad scam) in the back room of a Park Slope brownstone; a bunch of dockworkers playing cards and waiting for the "shape-up" in a Red Hook renovation. And so many more. And, I've also found more than one old lady spirit still toddling around a kitchen, waiting for her son to come back from a war. There is so often a war.

I don't advise taking on ghosts lightly. It can open doors you can have trouble shutting. But, if you take care of the energetic and physical (and therefore also energetic) aspects of your house, it can make a difference as to what and who wants to stay there.

Lightening up creates—lightening up.

TWENTY

Messages Are Everywhere

Some people find their intuitive messages in smoke, or at the bottom of a teacup. Some find them by talking to stones. Or by opening books at random. Many years ago, I got a single fortune cookie that had six identical messages stuffed inside, all saying, in essence, don't do that big thing you are planning to do tomorrow. I didn't listen. Turns out, the cookie—or whatever got it to my table—was giving me some very good advice.

When we don't listen, the messages can get louder. My first big intuitive messages were delivered by trucks. Early in the 1980s, I remember being worried about how something was going to work out. I was in the back of a cab, and suddenly rolling into my line of vision was a big green truck that read, "Mystic Oil."

I laughed and decided that this was a good sign. Everything indeed turned out fine, and I somehow chose to adopt these gorgeous green and gold trucks as my harbinger of good news.

What could be better than Mystic Oil? Every truck was so spotlessly clean and shining, it could have safely delivered unwrapped medical supplies. In over twenty years, I never saw one speck of dust on a Mystic Oil truck.

Late in the 1990s, when I wanted so much to make the switch to doing intuitive work, I heard a voice in my head when I was on the subway during the morning rush. It said, "Get off at the next stop." This represented a conflict. I was really early for once for my perma-lance job, and had planned to go into the office and noisily start the coffeepot.

But after a little deliberation, I thought, "This might be a test, and it might also be the real deal." So I got off. Then, I was sensing very specific instructions to go two blocks this way, three blocks that, and so forth. Suddenly, I found myself at the very edge of a teeming, windy highway. The voice commanded, "Look left NOW!" And there was a big, bright Mystic Oil truck barreling down the road.

In 2007, when I started teaching my drop-in course in intuition, I was walking briskly down West Tenth Street on the way to the school. That particular thoroughfare is little more than a small, curving country lane, trapped in the big city.

Yet, on February 14th, the night of my second class, I saw TWO huge Mystic Oil trucks come flying around those curves, one right after the other, rolling toward me. It was a good thing, too, because when I went to class that night, not one person showed up. It was Valentine's Day, after all—but because of the trucks, I was encouraged to keep going. And the course ultimately worked out beautifully.

One time, I was praying about a very difficult situation, and asked, "Please, God, please, move into it! I'm afraid I'm going to mess it up and lose all the things I need to keep. Please take it away from me." I thought it was odd to use the word, "move," and yet it also felt right. I needed that level of involvement.

Within thirty seconds, I turned the corner and looked up, and there was a truck I had never seen before. And here is what it said in big letters: "Divine Moving & Storage Ltd. We Have the Divine Touch." And on it was a picture of God reaching out to Adam, liberally borrowed from the Sistine Chapel.

You cannot ask for clearer than that. Well, you could, but I can't imagine what it would be, unless the truck also played "Leaning on the Everlasting Arms" in the cheerful, tinkling style celebrating a favorite soft-serve ice cream.

I think if you want a sign from the universe, the best thing to do is to begin to ask, and then observe. People might say that it is magical thinking. But I think it's a kind of dance between you and the various levels of reality. Why did I make that anguished plea to ask God to move in just as I was walking down that particular street? The problem had been plaguing me for days. As analytical psychologist C. G. Jung said, "In all chaos there is a cosmos, in all disorder a secret order." I think there's a give and take.

And you may not find that the medium of your message is the panel of a truck. It might be the kinds of birds that come into your yard at the moment you're looking out. Or the bits of nature that land on an outdoor table. Your messages might come with a little tingle of excitement just before you read a billboard.

Or you might find them over a coffee cup, rather than in the bottom of a teacup, as a friend just happens to answer the questions you haven't even asked yet. Or, you might hear that voice within that is strongest when we are quietest.

Even my messages are a little subtler now. I haven't seen a Mystic Oil truck in years. I just try to get quiet more often now and listen more carefully. Blessed is she who doesn't need a ton of steel to drive the message home.

TWENTY-ONE

Grab a Pocketful of Change

The universe is most likely to kiss us when we are on our unique path. The minute I suggest to people that they need to take seriously the idea of doing what they were born to do, they say, "But what about the money?" The consensus seems to be that if they could be guaranteed a smooth, easy financial experience, they'd get started at once. Otherwise, they'll forget it and go eat some ice cream. The lack of absolute assurance often appears to be the deal breaker.

It's like saying, "God never gives us more than we can handle." A wise woman once told me, "Of course God gives us more than we can handle. Why else would we need God?" (By the way, insert whatever you want here . . . higher mind, higher power, Great Spirit, none of the above, all of the above. I know from my childhood on the buckle of the Bible Belt that certain words may resonate oddly. If you have room for something—anything—higher than your own personality, it's very helpful.)

In this country, money is the great report card for our efforts. If we're making money, the popular notion is that our endeavors must be—and therefore we must be—legitimate and good. Goodness knows I was paid plenty to sell collectibles to people who clearly needed to spend their resources in more essential ways, or to save. I've seen films on credit abuse and watched through my fingers when I observed those selfsame collector plates on the walls of homes soon to be forcibly vacated.

This is the Calvinist ideal pulled through into some facets of the New Age. Big prosperity is part of the package—like Mr. and Mrs. Wallet's approach—and that may be your path. But many are going to have some financial ups and downs as we find our way to our soul's true purpose. This process develops sensory abilities, safe surrender, and soul-muscles you'll have forever.

My sense of it is that doing your purpose in life is the best health insurance you'll ever have.

My husband and I, when we were younger, loved to look at what we affectionately called "geezer videos" on PBS—documentaries about old people who were doing their purpose and enjoying it so much. These folks might have been a little stiff or bent over, but their eyes were clear and bright and fiery, and they were having fun. Now we're older, and just trying to emulate those geezers.

Some people have a romantic vision of telling off the boss, using their inflammatory memos as tinder for their bridges, and then starting their life's purpose. It doesn't need to happen that way. It doesn't need to be binary. It can be more like melted mozzarella.

You might keep working your job in the day, or part-time, but you can see it as a ticket to your true profession. Doing so typically downgrades the drama around it. As the job becomes less and less of your identity, you may develop a more detached approach to what goes on in the workplace. It's still important to work *well*, but you'll find that a lot of the craziness will release of its own accord because your eyes are also on the prize.

You might say, "I'm tired at the end of the day." Most people with jobs are being worked pretty hard, I know. But, some of the fatigue may also come from ignoring your life's purpose. Dig in, get started, and you may find new energy.

Bashar, the consciousness channeled by Darryl Anka, says that abundance is "The ability to do what you need to do when you need to do it, period." And he adds "Did you hear anything in that definition . . . about money?"

My Dad, who ran his rental service for thirty years, used to say, "You don't need a ¾-inch drill, you need a ¾-inch hole." What he meant is that certain things are a means to an end, but they are not the end in and of themselves.

Money helps you get shelter, food, clothing, and other things you want and need. But paying full price—or using money, period—is not the only way to acquire those things.

My husband is an excellent character actor who works primarily in independent films and on Off-Off Broadway. (Off-Off, though exciting theater, typically pays actors little if anything. At present, there's a particular project that may take him to remunerative Off-Broadway.) He is also a brilliantly nitpicky academic editor and grant writer who adds luster to scholarly reputations with his relentless fact checking and logic. On my side, nearly all my Reiki clients are referrals. I suggest they come back when it seems right for them, rather than committing them to a weekly schedule. I've always also done *pro bono* community work, which feels right. And yet, we have everything we need.

A few examples of how we did it:

⦿ In December 1993, four years before I discovered Reiki, our son was just over a year old, and my finances were almost tapped out. Months earlier, my advertising agency had been involved in a court case involving maternity leave, and, as a result, the choice I was given was to come back full-time or not at all. I opted for not at all. I learned that the stream of money I thought advertising would always offer me had an "off" position.

During the year after our son's birth, I had learned how to care for him, to find new clients and build a freelance practice in the hours our au pair took over (yes, I know that sounds glitzy, but it was a much more budget-friendly program in the early 1990s), and to deal with a postpartum depression. I was getting better at all of them, but money was tight.

Christmas was coming. My sister-in-law's birthday was coming. This was my very tall and beautiful sister-in-law, who had yet to meet her even taller husband. (Little did we know that he was just on the horizon.) I decided to give her a birthday brunch at home, to invite my in-laws, and to make it nice, but I couldn't afford flowers. So I started doing everything I could think to do—iron the nicest tablecloth and napkins, come up with an economical menu that was still elegant.

The day before the brunch, I walked past a funeral home and saw, in the gutter, one of those big fanlike floral tributes. There were fresh, gorgeous pink star-gazer lilies and milky white Bermuda lilies. I asked the man who had just dropped it—and I hadn't seen flowers dropped in the gutter before—"May I take this?" "Help yourself," he said. "Otherwise, it goes in the garbage."

Mentally thanking the person who inspired this floral arrangement, and the one who purchased it, I took it straight home, pulled it apart, rearranged the flowers, and had two beautiful displays—one for the living room, and one for the table. Everything looked great, my sister-in-law totally appreciated it, and the floral tribute had a second life.

Oddly enough, a few days after the brunch, I got a call to come into the agency and do some work. The court case had been resolved and I could work free-lance.

❂ Early on, I discovered the work of Amy Dacyczyn, editor of *The Tightwad Gazette*. Her ideas are ex-treme—she was raising six children to our one—and she actually once made a Frankenstein mask out of dryer lint. But her principles are excellent. It's like high fashion: you might not want to wear precisely what comes down the runway, but it may influence your color palette for the season.

◉ When our son was small, he looked like a princeling when we went out for special occasions. A neighbor's mother-in-law sent her grandsons handsome, well-made pants, sweaters, shirts, and navy wool blazers from Italy, and I made sure to show up early at every stoop sale for items they had outgrown.

◉ My husband was called in last-minute to replace a fellow actor in a star-studded reading about the Astor Place Riots. We all enjoyed the evening and met luminaries at the cocktail party after. Our son, aged five, engaged journalist and author Pete Hamill in a discussion about television.

◉ Early in my Reiki practice, I declared that I needed a little bread-and-butter work so that I could let my client relationships grow naturally, rather than under pressure. Three days later, I got a call to do some freelance writing for a French cooking school. *Voilà du pain et du beurre!*

One day there was a cooking demo, and our then eight-year-old son needed to come along because his school was out. He and I sat with the students in the culinary theater as the famed Chef André Soltner demonstrated his superb technique and simply radiated joy. Tasting plates were circulated. Our son passed on the fish, the chicken, and the vegetable, but when the delicate flanlike cake came around, he gladly accepted a portion and a spoon from a smiling student. "Eh, boy, *now* you eat!" called an amused Chef Soltner from the stage. And he directed students to wrap up a number of pieces of this exquisite dessert for our son in foil so thick, it could have covered the LEM lunar lander.

The day came, however, when I could bid the school a friendly and heartfelt *merci beaucoup et adieu,* and do Reiki exclusively, and that was good, too.

◉ I have found myself thinking idly that my face looked rather dry, only to find a sealed sample of good-quality moisturizer thrown into my front yard a couple of days later.

◉ A woman on a local email chain was getting married and wanted to divest herself of her old wardrobe. It was my size, and I accepted it gladly. Some of it was real single-girl clothing, designed to show off the goods, so to speak, so I passed that along to friends or charity. But the classic pieces I blessed and enjoyed. She and I still have coffee from time to time.

◉ I found a gorgeous African rattle in a clean cardboard box in front of a restaurant. I still use it.

❀ A major concern was how to pay for our son's college. We stuffed his college fund with every dollar we could spare. I encouraged (OK, nagged) him to get good grades, which annoyed him, but worked. He was accepted at a rigorous public high school from which he graduated with a high school diploma and an Associate's Degree. Two years of college at no charge. (I worked diligently on the school's fund-raising committee in thanks.) His chosen university accepted nearly all those credits and gave him a partial scholarship. He graduated with college money to spare. His internships turned into paid work combining two of his major loves in life. Now, he says, he also wants to take online courses to build his skill set and learn simply to learn, and not for grades. I totally appreciate and understand his thinking.

❀ My husband and I sometimes go to New England in summer to house-sit for our friends. Our week or ten days in this elegant "DIY B&B" generally runs around $300, including transportation from and to New York, a museum or two, a "thank you" present for and dinner with our hosts; another gift for our neighbors back home collecting our mail; a splurgy dinner for ourselves, and our other meals, most of which are cooked in the well-appointed kitchen from farmers' market specialties and enjoyed in a candlelit arbor. In addition, we water plants, and, on the last day, straighten things up and do laundry, so the tired world travelers can collapse into a fragrant, freshly made bed.

⊚ Even though I have more resources now, I find I can get the most elegant and well-made clothes at a fraction of their normal prices when I go to certain thrift shops in the Chelsea neighborhood of Manhattan. The unimaginable becomes totally wearable.

⊚ Some of our nicest art and most interesting furnishings started out as "mongo"—on-the-street finds that people responsibly leave out to be taken. One day I brought my husband a handsome mongo black polo shirt that had been artfully draped over a wrought iron fence, and he brought me a sidewalk-sourced bouquet of beautiful fresh white and gold Fiji mums, tied with a purple satin ribbon. It was a nice evening.

Sometimes, I really do splurge. A few years ago, I traveled in Northern India after presenting my work at an international conference in Delhi. Still, my friend and I stayed at ashrams rather than in luxury hotels, and we found that our accommodations were very good. We could have a beautiful, clean room with a view of the Ganges in the foothills of the Himalayas for $12.50 per person per night. I pick and choose. But I have more options to do so because I have made some conservative choices in other areas. Abundance.

There is an old story: a man tells a philosopher, "If you would just venerate the king, you wouldn't have to eat lentils." The philosopher replies, "If you would just eat lentils, you wouldn't have to venerate the king."

Would you rather have secondhand clothes, or a secondhand life?

TWENTY-TWO

Give Yourself Your Self

Sometime in the early 1980s, I was invited to give a Saturday workshop at a CUNY school on how to find a career to love, as part of a special day for young women in business.

We were all wearing these little foulard ties back then, and matched jackets and skirts in conservative cuts and colors, mostly like we were men with bumps. We wanted to be taken seriously. We were dedicated. Why, then, would I go out for drinks with someone and, within ten minutes, observe that she was weeping into her wasabi? Time and again, women told me that they were so disappointed in their jobs.

Now, I know that there were complicated issues at hand: women were hired with the promise of power, and then relegated to positions where the ceiling was never raised; we were just strung along financially; we hadn't been brought up at that time in the rough-and-tumble mentality of team sports; we had to work twice as hard to get begrudging recognition; many of us were first-generation women in corporations with no role models; the list went on and on.

Certain safeguards were not yet in place. I personally remember being called into an agency at 7:30 A.M. to review a presentation with the president of the firm. We were all alone. I knew something was going south when the president looked up at me through his hooded gray eyes below his gray shock of hair, and purred, "Sooooo . . . do you find me . . . attractive?" Before that, I had never understood why there was a shower installed in one of the restrooms on the floor.

I mentally borrowed my mother's Mom-ray, shot it at him, and barked, "We need to get this done! Client's coming at two!" It shut him up. And down.

Nevertheless, even then, I had this idea about an authentic life. So, I decided to create a workshop that would start with a guided meditation about a perfect day. My idea was to first elicit some of the underused talents and passions these women had. On their perfect day, might they spend hours reading? Making art? Hiking in the wilderness?

Then, I thought, we would brainstorm together about positions that used some aspect of this activity or talent so that women might see that there was a creative way to have a more authentic connection with their career. If we had time, we might even network together to help people find an informational interview, mentoring, or training. (This was well before the Internet was in our realm. Information was much harder to come by.)

Everyone in the classroom looked eager; there were twenty-somethings and thirty-somethings with their datebooks on the desktops, wearing the Saturday version of business wear, which usually meant jacketed pantsuits, knee-high nylon stockings, and elegant flats. By the end of the day, the toes of those knee-highs would get smelly and crunchy. We kept our shoes on.

I turned off the lights and began a guided meditation. "You are waking up on your perfect day. What do you have for breakfast? Now, you are doing exactly what you enjoy most on your perfect day. Where are you? What are you doing? What excites you about it?" and so I continued through the day. Then . . . I asked each student to take a few deep breaths . . . and bring her consciousness back fully into the room. I turned on the lights.

All around me were tear-stained faces. A woman raised her hand and said she'd spent her day sledding with her imaginary children. Her perfect day had been to wake up with her yet-to-be-met husband in a house in the country, with two kids, and a golden retriever. I saw lots of nods around the room.

"Well," I said, wondering what to do with this.

Sudden shouts of "STOP! STOP!" drew our attention to the hall. We heard a rapid "bam-bam-bam" footfall, the rhythm even faster down a flight of stairs, the screech of a metal door flying open, slamming shut. We opened our classroom door to learn that, while we were in the dark, someone had come up the stairs, bypassed us, gone into the adjoining classroom, demanded everyone's wallets, stuffed them into a backpack, and fled.

The commotion brought other people into the hall. Everyone wanted to know why the thief hadn't hit our classroom first. "Oh," I said, "The lights were out. We were meditating on our perfect day." The crime victims just rolled their eyes.

There wasn't a lot we could do, having seen nothing of the wallet snatcher himself. So, we closed the door and went back to our discussion. "Well," I said, as a breathtakingly insensitive segue to our work, "You can see that seeking the truth pays off." Horrible.

In some cases, the women were ashamed as they shared their domesticated visions of a perfect day. But I continued, "At least if you know this about yourself, that your idea of perfection is a husband and family, you will recognize why there's a certain dissonance in how you think you should feel about your work, and how you do. On this we can build."

That was then. What amazes me is that even today, some young people who work with me still see part of their life as stuck because they don't have that perfect, consuming relationship. It's as if they are holding some of their breath all of the time.

I am not dissing this type of relationship. There are people who really do seem to get it. I read about them in the "Vows" section of *The New York Times*. Of course, I also read the "Vows" updates to follow up on "happily ever after."

If you think that life's central joy and meaning is going to be realized *only* through the long-term connection with another specific person, it's my opinion that there's going to be a bit of desperation in and around your process. So many people put that relationship in the slot where something else belongs: discovery of what they truly love, what brings them joy, what they came to do. You see, the other person should be doing the same thing for herself or himself, rather than being the primary source of what makes your life meaningful.

And if you won't give yourself what you need, why should that other person? If you won't give yourself love and consideration, then you walk around with the energetic profile of being unloved. Frankly, that profile may seem unattractive to a balanced potential partner.

The brilliant Jamie Sams, who coauthored those cool *Medicine Cards* and wrote *Dancing the Dream*, stated that in her Native American tradition, the first relationship is with the Divine, the second is with the self, and all others follow.

Certainly, many of our internalized rules about not giving ourselves what we want and need come from the programming of early childhood, much of which may be forgotten or buried.

What we have survived in the past becomes part of our survival script. This is an evolutionary glitch. Sometimes the best way to deal with the thicket of your history is to cut your own path by doing the very things that were outlawed in your family of origin—like putting yourself at the center of your own life.

Parts of you only feel safe enforcing past rules. Let them discover that you can not only do something new and live to tell the tale, but laugh too.

Dr. Lawrence LeShan, the noted research and clinical psychologist, discovered many years ago that when cancer patients who were considered terminal started to respond to their desire to do some very simple things they had always wanted to do—even things like learning to play piano, just for themselves, so as to give their life more meaning, hope, and fulfillment—their likelihood of survival increased dramatically. *Cancer as a Turning Point* should be required reading for every cancer patient, in my estimation.

From a homeopathic perspective, I learned from Dr. Rudolph Ballentine's *Radical Healing* that there are three levels of potentials for disease, and they are all linked with our life's mission.

At the first level, we resist our own mission and itch to do something that is not really right for us. And that's associated with problems of the skin—generally involving a fair amount of scratching or trying not to.

At the second level, we've given up what it is we came to do, and just given in to too much of everything—too much food, staying up too late, too much booze, too many collector dolls. Disease progresses into the mucus membranes, and there is also overconstruction—so we get lumps and bumps, too much hair, and often too much weight.

At the third level, it's clear that the we are not going to do what we came to do. So the body begins to erode. Nature is efficient.

It's not to say that there are not other factors involved in disease, including in cancer—there are plenty of them. But this is ground-level stuff, just as in the idea that the kind of bacteria that grows in a petri dish will tell you something of the culture medium.

If you want to pull back to a wider perspective, remember that the Irish say (well, some Irish, anyway), "There are no pockets in a shroud." If there are indeed many lives, about all we can take along are our experiences, our talents, our connections, and our own guided process in healing our karma and keeping our promises about what we came to do.

Your ideal bucket list might not involve one day of hang gliding in Madagascar, but rather years of tap dancing beyond shuffle-ball-change; becoming a lot more patient; finally learning French and going to France; nurturing a relationship with a friend with strangely familiar eyes; and discovering that part of you is satisfied when you help the elderly, so clearing your neighbor's walk or weeding her flowers becomes a regular practice. These are steady life enhancements. My brilliant brother, a computer engineer, created a greenhouse where he can show his grandsons how a juicy tomato comes to be.

What did you come to do? That's your burden, your joy, that's your process. Hopefully, these stories have helped you and will continue to help you understand how to listen and observe, how to try and sense and course-correct.

Some day, every one of us will pass into spirit. That's what my young artist friend told me in 1970 when I said, "Why do you keep planning your funeral? Why not your wedding?" She would come to me with sketches of streamlined red fiberglass coffins, very cool, like a surfboard to the Beyond. "I don't know that I'm going to get married," she said. "I do know that I'm going to die." But she did get married. She had two children, and taught at the local school. Everything looked great—at least in the Christmas letters printed on thick, festive paper. After many years, her husband left her for someone else. She got cancer. Then, she began to get excited about small boats and started a river-based delivery service. She got better. Maybe all those coffins she drew were really watercraft.

I believe that when we do pass over, the luminous, beautiful, brilliant beings we meet are not going to ask us where we got our shoes, or how many apps we have on our various devices, or who we last saw at the nearest mega-arena. I bet they don't profile us on how we spent our Sundays, what we last tweeted, or whether we consider ourselves lactose intolerant, or even vegan. My sense is that they will ask us something like this:

"How did you spend that fabulous gift, your life?

"Did you accomplish what you set out to do?

"Did you reflect and radiate your authentic self?

"Did you gain in compassion, love, empathy, strength?

"Did you truly add to the love in the world?

"Is your soul at rest because your soul work is good for now?"

In the meantime, as a Hopi elder once said, "Those who are at peace in their hearts already are in the great shelter of life."

Love to you, now and always!

Eleven Ways to Be Kissed and Tell It!

1. Eat calmer, quieter food. The average four-ounce fast-food burger contains morsels of fifty-five to over a thousand different cows. That's a lot of energy of misery to take in. Go for more plants, as pesticide-free as possible. We get information of all kinds via our first brain (third eye) and our second brain (gut).

2. Have a daily practice—chanting, meditating, praying, breathing, moving quietly. It doesn't matter so much what you do as much as how consistently you do it. As my adorable sister says about overcoming obstacles, "Do it first thing! Don't do anything else before you do it!" Ask to be guided. Get quiet, ready to hear or see or even sense or taste or pick up an aroma. Into my Reiki room come spirit healers who deliver spirit herbal medicine, and my clients can taste it.

3. Be a little nicer to everyone than you're used to. Be as kind and considerate to the student as the teacher, to the housekeeper as the employer, to the newsdealer as to your nearest and dearest, and vice versa. This doesn't mean being a doormat—just openhearted.

Be nice, too, to the people who really irritate you, because they really are showing you disowned parts of yourself.

4. Pay attention. Are you starting to see a lot of any particular image on the streets, in the media, even in shop windows, at friends' houses, and on tote bags? Look up its meaning, or, better yet, ask why it would be calling your attention. Repeated numbers also qualify.

5. Take a breath. When you are starting to behave in habitual ways that don't work, take a breath. Ask your guides for a better way to go. Try something new.

6. Dream, dream, dream. Ask to be guided in your dreams. If you want to connect with someone who has passed, ask before sleep to meet that person on the astral plane in your dreams. You might not remember the meeting, but note how you feel in the morning.

7. Create a little space in your house that is consistently used for meditation or connection with the higher forces. Burn sage, incense, candles. Put images that inspire you there, too.

8. Be willing to empty your teacup. Tea can't flow into a full cup without making a mess. Create a space to learn something new; punch a hole in your old, tired stories about how everything is.

9. Take a "Happiness Snapshot." Is the coffee good this morning? Was the shower warm? Good! Acknowledge that! When you don't get everything you want, think of the things you didn't get that you really didn't want. Say "thank you," a lot. The guides will eventually start responding.

10. Notice the activities that make you feel more happy and alive on the planet. They are hints.

11. Recognize that whatever you are doing is being written in light. Do your best!

What do we mean by "do your best?" Earth is the planet of distraction. We incarnate with a list of souls to see and troubles to repair, but we get distracted . . . there are sooo many distractions. It becomes like high-stakes gambling: you can burn a lot of bad karma here quickly, but it's also quite easy to mess things up.

Imagine, for instance, that we meet one of the souls we hurt deeply in what we call a past life, and promised, this time, we'd honor and love them. It's an agreement made from both sides before birth. This can happen between parents and children, too. Or we encounter situations that don't involve the original souls, but resonate with a past life in some important way.

We might start off consciously and well, but as we react to familiar energy, we repeat the very behaviors we were to amend in the first place. We not only fail to clear the karma, we make more.

This, I believe, is why some relationships feel particularly devastating when they don't work out—it's the loss of a soul opportunity as well as a love.

One answer is to be much more conscious in all our relationships. If you knew your behavior was being written in light, what would you do?

If you've truly blown it, you can repair some karma, even if you never get back together permanently. You find the person, admit to your wrongdoing, and ask what would make it right. "I'm sorry" is not enough. "I'm sorry" is all about you. Change your focus.

Then, pay back the money; return the car repaired; paint the living room you always said you'd paint; speak to the friends to whom you dissed your partner; buy a lot of groceries—whatever it is, you are equal to the task. As you clean things up, your vibration (and heart) will become lighter. You will set the stage for higher guidance and better things.

One Last Kiss

Don't be surprised if the guides use humor to get you off your old position. In the early 1980s, I saw myself as a brainiac and spiritually evolving, despite the fact that my personal life was in a shambles. My guides were always trying to move me off overemphasis on my mind.

Before I went to bed one night, I asked my guides to send me to the kind of class in my sleep that would be right for me now. I imagined that, as I drifted off, I would find myself in an esoteric school, studying an ancient text full of mysterious symbols, while a Celtic harp played softly in the background. The walls would be encrusted with crystals, I would give the group an interpretation they'd never considered before . . . blahdy blah blah . . . blah blah.

Imagine my surprise, then, when the class of my dreams—and in my dreams—turned out to be roller skating! I saw myself in a purple and white tweed cape, a brisk wind to my back, flying down some very bumpy pavement, just barely able to keep my silly white skates parallel! They were roller rink skates, yet here they were on the rough concrete. All theory. My arms were lurching, my knees locked, and it was clear that I was not managing well.

I was so disappointed at the time—but what a hilarious way to tell me that I needed balance!

In about the same era, I was in a room filled with people meditating, perhaps in a seminar run by Mr. Wallet, and the energy was really flowing. The meditative images I was seeing on my mental screen resembled those I had read about in near-death experiences.

I seemed to be moving through a tunnel to an energy field of unconditional love and light. I wanted to get closer. As I approached this gorgeous, pastel-colored vibration of perfect harmony, a figure emanating brilliant color stepped in the way, blocking my view.

The figure said to me, "Would you like to know the secret of the universe?"

Would I! Now we were finally getting somewhere.

"Yes, please," I said, with all the humility I could muster.

The guide paused for effect, then intoned solemnly: "A-wop-bom-a-loo-mop-a-lomp-bam-boom!"

Embrace It All

Write about a time when you felt guided and loved from out of the blue.

_____

_____

_____

_____

_____

_____

_____

_____

_____

_____

_____

_____

_____

_____

What was the most remarkable part of that experience?

_____

_____

_____

_____

_____

_____

_____

What did it ultimately teach you?

_____

_____

_____

_____

_____

_____

Where do you need guidance, help, and love from out of the blue today?

_____

_____

_____

_____

_____

_____

What can you do from your side to encourage it?

_____

_____

_____

_____

_____

_____

_____

When you are at the end of your life, what do you want to have accomplished?

_____

_____

_____

_____

_____

What do you want to be remembered for?

_____

_____

_____

_____

_____

What will you take through time?

_____

_____

_____

_____

_____

_____

_____

What needs to happen now to start or enhance this process?

_____

_____

_____

_____

_____

_____

_____

CPSIA information can be obtained
at www.ICGtesting.com
Printed in the USA
FFOW04n1925221114